What About My Husband, Lord?

Encouragement and Wisdom For Single and Married Women

Mary Turek

WESTBOW
PRESS
A DIVISION OF THOMAS NELSON

Unless otherwise indicated, Bible quotations are taken from the Amplified Bible, Old Testament copyright © 1965, 1987 by the Zondervan Corporation. The Amplified New Testament copyright © 1958, 1987 by The Lockman Foundation. Used by permission.

(There is one scripture taken from the New International Version.)
Scripture taken from the Holy Bible, New International Version
Copyright © 1973, 1978, 1984 by International Bible Society. Used by permission of Zondervan Publishing House. All rights reserved.

WestBow Press books may be ordered through booksellers or by contacting:

WestBow Press
A Division of Thomas Nelson
1663 Liberty Drive
Bloomington, IN 47403
www.westbowpress.com
1-(866) 928-1240

ISBN: 978-1-4497-1831-2 (sc)
ISBN: 978-1-4497-1833-6 (hc)
ISBN: 978-1-4497-1832-9 (e)

Library of Congress Control Number: 2011930621

Printed in the United States of America

WestBow Press rev. date: 6/13/2011

For my husband, Joe. You are my perfect match, and I'm so thankful to the Lord that He chose you for me. Your love has been a protective covering from the enemy's arrows. I'm waiting with anticipation to see every promise of the Lord demonstrated in our life together and thankful for every day that I have been your wife.

To the memory of my father, Dr. Robert C. Barnard or as I always referred to him, "Daddy." He so magnificently modeled the unconditional and sacrificial love of my Heavenly Father, it was easy to know in my heart that we are truly the apple of His eye and it is His delight to bring blessing and provision into every detail of our lives. Daddy, you taught me to determine to set my forehead like flint with the Word in my heart that I can do all things through Christ Who strengthens me. You stood with me in faith believing for God to bring my God-chosen husband until your promotion to heaven and I know you were watching, as part of the great cloud of witnesses, with tears of thanksgiving when I walked down the aisle to become Mrs. Joseph Turek.

Table of Contents

Foreword

As a director and minister of a healing ministry, I have had the opportunity to hear the hearts of many single women who are believing God for the mate that He has chosen for their lives. I have heard the hearts of married women who are praying and believing for their husband to walk in the maturity and victory that God has for them. I would like to commend my good friend and ministry partner, Mary Turek, for allowing the Holy Spirit to use her life as an example to others. The direction and encouragement she gives through the Word and her own personal life in this book brings hope in hopeless situations.

Larry Duncan
Director of Guiding Light Ministries Healing Rooms

I considered it an honor when Mary Turek asked me to write a foreword for her book. Mary states in her book that if you take your eyes off Jesus and you're not trusting in Him, you will take things into your own hands.

In Mary's quest to allow the Lord to choose her mate for her I never once saw or knew of a time when she took her eyes off Jesus and did not trust Him for her future.

Mary was truly a sign and a wonder as I watched her through the years wait on God for her mate. She never wavered in her trust in the Lord to complete His promise of choosing a husband for her.

I remember the Prophetic Word that was given to Mary from Sandy Powell at our Women's Retreat, March 2002. I remember the Gold Dust that the Holy Spirit released while Mary was sharing her testimony. The presence of the Holy Spirit was thick in the room as she spoke.

If there ever was a truly modern-day Proverbs 31 woman it would be Mary. Proverbs 31:10 states "Who can find a virtuous wife?" V.11: "The heart of her husband safely trusts in her."

Mary is that virtuous woman in Proverbs and as I have observed, her husband safely trusts in her. He cannot speak of Mary without honoring her in every way.

Mary knows what it's like to be single and knows what it's like to be married. She lives what she has written. One may call her a walking epistle read of all men.

The advice Mary is giving to all women is not a clanging symbol or a sounding brass. In other words, she's not just making noises, she has lived her advice that is to let God choose your mate and trust Him to do just that.

With all this said, I might add that Mary is one of the kindest and most loving persons that I know. When you read her book it will testify of this.

Dr. Anita F. Mason L.M.S.T.: D. Min.
Joshua Company Ministries

Acknowledgements

Thanks...

to Larry Duncan who followed God's prompting in encouraging me to publish what God has given me for other women.

to Gloria Kirby, who spent days editing and proofing this book. Your enthusiasm spurred me to write about my God-adventures. Without your input, this work would not have fully been what God intended it to be.

to the many who played an invaluable roll in my God-adventures, for allowing me to share part of *your* story as well as mine.

Part 1

What About My Husband, Lord?

Encouragement and Wisdom
For The Single Woman

Introduction

What About My Husband, Lord?

Encouragement and Wisdom
For The Single Woman

When a single woman asks the Lord, *"What about my husband?"* she is saying, "Who is he? Where is he? When is he coming? And why isn't he here yet?" God is the one who made you with a natural desire to have a husband and a family, and He is willing and able to choose just the right mate and bring him to you in His perfect timing.

God wants to be your match-maker! *What About My Husband, Lord? Encouragement and Wisdom For The Single Woman* addresses what you need to know and do (and not do) to receive all that God has for you in this area.

God took me on an amazing journey that started with the discovery that He was willing to be my match-maker and ended with a trip down the aisle to become one with my God-chosen husband, Joe. The lessons I learned through this faith walk, I gratefully share in these pages. God is faithful and He understands our weaknesses. He is always ready to give us the encouragement and strength to believe Him as we put our lives in His hands, so He can do whatever is needed to meet those God given desires. He is the King of Kings and Lord of Lords, but He is also your Abba – your daddy who loves you immeasurably and unconditionally. He longs for you to trust Him enough to let Him bring you, His daughter, the most perfect match into your life to be your husband and soul mate.

And this is the confidence (the assurance, the privilege of boldness) which we have in Him: [we are sure] that if we ask anything (make any request) according to His will (in agreement with His own plan), He listens to and hears us.

And if (since) we [positively] know that He listens to us in whatever we ask, we also know [with settled and absolute knowledge] that we have [granted us as our present possessions] the requests made of Him.

1 John 5:14, 15

Chapter 1

It Started With A Prayer

I was 28 years old and was enthralled with my job as a first grade teacher, but I knew I was ready to make the change. I was ready to move into my new role as a wife and a mother – something I had wanted since I was a very young girl. I had considered every adjustment that I imagined would come with this new life because I was about to make a request to God for it. Just in case the answer came next week in the form of a first date with my husband, it was important that I knew that I was really ready now. So with the realization that yes, I did want it now, I sat up in my bed, and there in the dark, made a simple request to the Lord for a husband, knowing that if I asked for one, I would have one. God heard and answered that prayer, but His sense of time is definitely not in sync with mine! Had I known the wait that was before me, I would have despaired. His ways are not our ways, but God knows best!

What I expected was that through the dating process, my husband and I would meet, fall in love and realize that we were right for each other. God had something *better* in mind!

The Darkness Is Defeated By Our Praise

Four years had passed since the prayer for a husband, and I was in deep pain over the break-up of a relationship that I had hoped would lead to marriage. God saw, and what He was about to do in response to my sorrow would make Him more real to me than ever before. Whether a dream or a vision, I do not know. In bed, in the dark, I could hear the powers of darkness in the hallway, laughing and gloating over my loss. They had gotten me good! I looked up and saw a small circle of light in the center of the bedroom ceiling. I knew in my heart that it was the light of the Lord. I raised my hands and praised Him with thanksgiving pouring out of my heart, that He was my shield, my refuge, my strong tower, my help in times of trouble, my deliverer, that I was more than a conqueror through Him who loves me, that He was my way-maker and my Faithful And True. And as the praise poured from my heart to Him who is Lord over all, the circle of light flooded across the ceiling and down the walls until the entire room was engulfed in light. At that instant, the powers of darkness were silenced and gone.

Two months later, while on my way to my summer school classroom, I turned on the radio in my car to listen to a Christian station for the first time, having just recently learned about the station's existence. A song was already in progress. The first words that I heard, "Never believe what you hear in the night. Keep your eyes on Jesus, and visions of light will come flooding over you," filled the car. I would later learn that it was a song by Harvest called *His Angels Are Everywhere.* God had given someone a song that narrated my exact experience from two months before! I couldn't stop crying tears of joy that God had sent me a crystal clear message that He cared deeply about my pain. For years afterward, I would share the story of that experience – a message for all that the powers of darkness cannot stay in the presence of true praise coming from His people. He had opened up my spiritual eyes, so that I could actually see what happens when we turn our eyes to Him, and ignore the circumstances which may be fact, and choose to speak the truth, His Word, which will change the facts to line up with the truth.

I believe that this experience was a key factor in the supernatural way that the Lord chose to answer my request for a husband. Restoration that was started through those praises was fully birthed on my wedding day, when I said, "I do!"

God has always been in the restoration business. When God restores, what you gain is more than what you would have had, originally. Have you suffered devastation in your husband-situation? Whether single or married, God can restore. Look to the Lord, commit your way to Him and send out your praises! If you are single, there is more good news. God is the match-maker!

The Lord, the God of heaven, Who took me from my father's house, from the land of my family and my birth, Who spoke to me and swore to me, saying, To your offspring I will give this land—He will send His Angel before you, and you will take a wife from there for my son.

Genesis 24:7

Chapter 2

God Is The Match-Maker!

How wonderful it would have been to have that valuable piece of information as a young woman, and how much grief and turmoil would I have been spared! It says in God's Word, that "my people perish for lack of knowledge" (Hosea 4:6) and this was an area in which I was living far from the abundant life that God promised. I did eventually come to know that God was able and willing to choose a mate just right for me, identify me to him as being his wife, identify him to me as being my husband, and bring us together. By God's grace, I experienced that blessing in exactly that manner without any dating involved. That part of my story will be told in detail in chapters four and five. My God-chosen husband and I began spending time together once we knew that God had chosen us to be husband and wife. With that knowing, God instantly and supernaturally filled us with a deep love for each other every bit as wonderful as I'd seen in my favorite romantic movies. God surely knows and wants to meet the desires of our hearts. When I came to the understanding that God is the match-maker, He gave me the grace to entrust Him completely with that area of my life. He took every step of this journey of faith with me, supplying me with the encouragement that I needed to be able to continue to the end. If you are a single woman who is desiring a husband, God will be your matchmaker too. He is no respecter of persons. He needs only to be asked. Let my experience encourage you that you can trust God with your hopes and dreams, and it is His joy and good pleasure to meet your deepest heart's desires.

Marriage is God's idea as shown in the scriptures:

Now the Lord God said, It is not good (sufficient, satisfactory) that the man should be alone; I will make him a helper meet (suitable, adapted, complementary) for him.

And out of the ground the Lord God formed every [wild] beast *and* living creature of the field and every bird of the air and brought them to Adam to see what he would call them; and whatever Adam called every living creature, that was its name.

And Adam gave names to all the livestock and to the birds of the air and to every [wild] beast of the field; but for Adam there was not found a helper meet (suitable, adapted, complementary) for him.

And the Lord God caused a deep sleep to fall upon Adam; and while he slept, He took one of his ribs *or* a part of his side and closed up the [place with] flesh.

And the rib *or* part of his side which the Lord God had taken from the man He built up *and* made into a woman, and He brought her to the man.

Then Adam said, This [creature] is now bone of my bones and flesh of my flesh; she shall be called Woman, because she was taken out of a man.

Therefore a man shall leave his father and his mother and shall become united *and* cleave to his wife, and they shall become one flesh.

Genesis 2:18-24

God not only ordained marriage, but also has given us clear guidelines in His Word to give us the understanding that enables us to walk in victory in this relationship. Jesus lets us know in John 10:10 that He came so we may have and enjoy life, and have it in abundance (to the full till it overflows). In order for you to have that enjoyable life in your marriage, you definitely need to be married to someone who is right for you. Who, more than the God Who made you and knows you intimately, would be more able to know exactly what you need and want in a mate in order to have a happy and successful marriage? How many times have you thought that someone was right for you only to be bitterly disappointed? It had happened to me and to some who had thought I would be right for them as well. Either way, it was disheartening to say the least. As God revealed His truth to me, I knew that He had a far better way that would be free of the pain and confusion that I had been experiencing.

The revelation that God would like to be my match-maker first came when reading Derek Prince's book ¹*God Is A Match-Maker*. It is the testimony of Derek's experience of having God identify Lydia, his first wife, to him as being his wife and bringing the two together. After a wonderful marriage with Lydia, who was 15 years Derek's senior, God identified Ruth to Derek, who was then a widower as being his second wife. The book was also partially written by Ruth, who shares their match-making experience from her perspective. For both of Derek Prince's marriages, the Lord identified husband and wife to each other as His choice for a mate, put love in their hearts for each other and brought them together under his direction and orchestration. Derek Prince did not date either one of his wives before their marriage to see if this was the one for him. As he put it, God put the knowledge that this was his wife " in a place in his heart where doubt had no access." So the time spent together before their marriage was for the purpose of preparing for marriage. Wow! This was the better way that I knew had to be God's plan for me! No more pain and confusion! Simply put the whole husband-situation in God's hands and let Him do it. Knowing that it isn't possible for God to make a mistake, and not being a risk taker, putting God in charge of the husband department especially made sense to me because that made getting the right match a sure thing. Little did I know how many valuable lessons the Lord had for me on the journey ahead, one of which was learning that my times are in His hands and my schedule is not the same as His. But God is never late and His timing is perfect. Trust in the Lord with all your heart and lean not on your own understanding (Proverbs 3:5). God used this adventure to teach me to walk in that Word and to be far better equipped for other situations later in life.

One advantage that worked mightily in my favor was that I had had the experience of being unconditionally loved by a wonderful earthly father. I knew what it was like to be the apple of my dad's eye. I knew what it was like to walk in the confidence that there was nothing that my earthly father wouldn't do to make my life better. No sacrifice would have been too big. Because of the blessing of a dad who had so well represented the love of my Heavenly Father, I understood that what God had done for Derek, He would do for me. So armed with the testimony from Derek Prince's life, and being fully persuaded that my Heavenly Father was able and willing to be my personal match-maker, I was ready to start on the new plan. No dating ever again! Ask God to identify my husband and me to each other as being husband and wife and bring us together, and then wait and trust. That was the new plan – a plan that came to completion only through God's grace and provision. It was His gift of faith, His ability to "fill my knower" – (my words to describe putting the knowledge in my heart in a place where doubt had no access), and His leading, protection and encouragement that empowered me to run the race. I, frankly, had nothing to offer in my own ability to reach the goal. At the beginning of this trip, I was often double-minded, impatient, and lacking understanding about what all was needed to walk in victory. This is a story about God's faithfulness. He is able! You are not! So quit striving and turn things over to your Heavenly Father. You are the apple of His eye and it is His delight to be your match-maker. His name is I Am because He is all you need. His name is Faithful And True because He will never fail you. Who better to trust with this deep desire of your heart?

God Was Isaac's Match-Maker

God has given us an account in His Word that shows He is the match-maker. It is detailed in Genesis when Abraham wanted a wife for his son Isaac. He called for his servant, Eliezer and had him swear by the Lord of heaven that he would not take a wife for Isaac from the Canaanite people, but that he would journey to the country of Abraham's relatives and take a wife for Isaac and bring her back for him. Abraham said that the Angel of the Lord would go before him, indicating that the Lord would prepare the way and set everything in place for Eliezer to make the right connections and come home with the wife that God had chosen for Isaac.

When Eliezer arrived at the land of Abraham's relatives, he prayed for a divine appointment with Isaac's soon-to-be wife and that God would clearly show him that this was she.

And he said, O Lord, God of my master Abraham, I pray You, cause me to meet with good success today and show kindness to my master Abraham.

See, I stand here by the well of water, and the daughters of the men of the city are coming to draw water.

And let it so be that the girl to whom I say, I pray you, let down your jar that I may drink, and she replies, Drink, and I will give your camels drink also – let her be the one whom you have selected *and* appointed *and* indicated for Your servant Isaac [to be a wife to him]; and by it I shall

know that You have shown kindness *and* faithfulness to my master.

Before he had finished speaking, behold, out came Rebekah, who was the daughter of Bethuel son of Milcah, who was the wife of Nahor the brother of Abraham, with her water jar on her shoulder.

Genesis 24:12-15

Rebekah's response to Eliezer, Abraham's servant, confirmed to him that she was Isacc's God-chosen wife and after spending time with her family and relaying his story to them, God also filled Rebekah's brother and father with a knowing that this was of the Lord, which gave them complete peace about being in agreement with the match.

Then Laban and Bethuel answered, The thing comes forth from the Lord; we cannot speak bad or good to you.

Genesis 24:50

The Lord had prepared Rebekah's heart and had given her peace, as well. When her family called to her and asked her what she wanted to do, she said that she would go. Her family spoke blessings over her union with Isaac, and then Rebekah and her maids followed Abraham's servant on their camels.

When the Lord identifies your spouse to you, you will be led by a complete peace that "this comes forth from the Lord" (as God did for Rebekah and her family) and that He is doing everything needed to bring the full work about. That peace the Lord will give you will relieve you from feeling the need to do something yourself to make it happen. Having God's complete peace is a key attribute of knowing that you have heard something from Him. That complete peace will help you to distinguish between hearing something out of your own spirit and thinking it is the Lord, and authentically having been informed by God. You will see later, as I share my testimony, how this component of peace in "having my knower filled" was the identifying factor of having God's fingerprints on it as He moved me into position to meet my husband and identified my husband to me.

Notice that after Abraham's servant prayed and put the situation in God's hands, God orchestrated his meeting with Isaac's intended wife so they were both at the right place at the right time. As you turn your husband-situation over to God, He will cause you and your husband to be in the right place at the right time for your appointed meeting. He won't allow you to miss it.

> **Now Isaac had returned from going to the well Beer-la-hai-roi [A well to the Living One Who sees me], for he [now] dwelt in the South country (the Negeb).**
>
> **And Isaac went out to meditate *and* bow down [in prayer] in the open country in the evening; and he looked up and saw that, behold, the camels were coming.**
>
> **And Rebekah looked up, and when she saw Isaac, she dismounted from the camel.**
>
> **For she [had] said to the servant, Who is that man walking across the field to meet us? And the servant [had] said, He is my master. So she took a veil and concealed herself with it.**
>
> **And the servant told Isaac everything that he had done.**
>
> **And Isaac brought her into his mother Sarah's tent, and he took Rebekah and she became his wife, and he loved her; thus Isaac was comforted after his mother's death.**
>
> **Genesis 24:62-67**

Isaac and Rebekah never dated. Neither did they need or try to do anything to cause their match to come about. It was literally a match made in heaven. As God "selected, appointed and indicated" (identified His choice) as quoted from Genesis 12:14, in the story of Isaac and Rebekah, He also did for me. He will do the same for you!

For You cause my lamp to be lighted, and to shine; the Lord my God illumines my darkness.

For by You I can run through a troop, and by my God I can leap over a wall.

As for God, His way is perfect! The word of the Lord is tested and tried; He is a shield to all those who take refuge and put their trust in Him.

Psalm 18:28-30

Chapter 3

Overcoming Obstacles To Faith
In The Process Of Waiting On The Lord

The enemy of our souls comes to steal, kill and destroy. But for every pitfall set before us, God has provision to position us to walk in victory. This is a look at the obstacles that were set before me in my faith walk to believe for God to be my match-maker, and the account of His faithfulness in causing me to overcome them all. God made me to understand that it was a desire of His heart to see me realize the desires of mine, and if I would entrust Him completely with the job, He would do whatever it took to cause me to go from barely hanging on, to waiting with that peace that passes understanding. The wind and the waves become irrelevant when you "know that you know" the One who calms the sea is in charge.

Shielded From Confusion – Having A Guarded Heart

Meditating on a promise in scripture until you are fully persuaded of its truth for you personally, positions you to move forward in faith. I absolutely had to know that God would never again allow me to walk in the confusion of thinking that someone was my husband who wasn't. Without total peace that God was my shield from that kind of confusion, I couldn't be in faith about Him bringing my desire of marrying my God-chosen husband to pass. God used this scripture to free me from that fear:

I will listen [with expectancy] to what God the Lord will say, for He will speak peace to His people, to His saints (those who are in right standing with Him)—but let them not turn again to [self-confident] folly.

Psalm 85:8

Confidently and wrongly believing that someone is your God-chosen husband, who really isn't, is certainly folly! This was the promise that guaranteed me God's protection from ever making that mistake again. During my fourteen-year journey of waiting for God to bring my husband, I frequently reminded myself and thanked Him, that He was shielding me from that painful mistake. As I believed, spoke and prayed that scripture in prayers of thanksgiving, the faith that I was safe from that error became unshakeable! Part of that promise speaks of the peace that God will impart to us that protects us from self-confident folly. That peace is a sign of having our knowers filled, or having God impart knowledge into our hearts in a place in which doubt has no access.

I asked the Lord to guard my heart, but I also realized that it was my job to do some things to guard my heart as well. In order to keep the door completely closed to developing any feelings for someone that God hadn't identified as my husband, I had a simple rule to which there were no exceptions. Until my husband was identified to me, I would not spend time alone with any man. That meant not going out for lunch or anything else. As far as I was concerned, no man was my husband until God had identified him to me as being such, and I would not allow myself to entertain any thoughts to the contrary about anyone. This rule kept my emotions safe from feelings that can come unexpectedly that lead to an emotional attachment or a hope that could cause disappointment, or even worse, cause me to leave God's path and marry the wrong man. I knew if I did my part, God would do His. In following that rule, I was making a decision concerning dating that set myself completely apart in lifestyle from the rest of the world of singles. I was also making it clear to the Lord that either He was going to completely make this whole thing happen, or it wasn't going to happen. I was determined to keep my hands off of it because I so desperately wanted to receive all that I knew He had for me.

Set Free From Doubt and Unbelief

At the beginning of my faith walk, at times I struggled. I knew in my heart that God was able and willing to do what I was trying to believe Him for, but frequently I knew that I wasn't standing in faith for what I knew He would do, if only I was standing in faith! I was walking in the confusion of double-mindedness between faith and doubt and feeling pretty miserable about it.

God heard my cries for help and He answered me through a prophetic word and a dream. One weekend, a prophetess came to minister at some services at my church. While standing up at the front of the sanctuary waiting for prayer, she gave me a word that I was trying to quit on something and run out the back door. But, Jesus wouldn't let me and He was holding the door shut tight. She told me also, that she knew that I didn't know what any of this meant, but that God would show me.

Because of my faith struggle, when I knew that someone may be coming to minister at church who may give me a word concerning my husband, I got myself worked up into a "stew" and was focused on my misery, not having my eyes on Jesus at all. In spite of wanting to demand as soon as the prophetess delivered the word, "Does this have anything to do with my husband or not!" God was very understanding and merciful! Unbeknownst to me at the time, He started something through that prophetic word that delivered me from all doubt about the husband-issue permanently.

Several weeks after being given that word, I had a dream in which I was in my apartment involved in spiritual struggles, over which I was gaining gradual victory. In the kitchen, the sink faucet was lifting by itself (which I knew in my dream indicated demonic interference) so I was taking authority over it in the name of Jesus. As I commanded it to turn off, it would. It came on again several times, but each time I used my spiritual authority and the Lord caused me to prevail. Then I looked in the direction of my bathroom and saw that the door was closed but the light was on. Knowing that I was home alone, I knew this wasn't going to be good news either. Upon opening the bathroom door, I saw bat-like creatures on the walls that I commanded to leave in the name of Jesus, as which time they all flew out and disappeared. The next thing I heard was the heavy creaking of something coming down the stairs. I knew in my spirit that it was very big and overwhelming – too big for me to handle. So I decided to quit and run out the back door to escape. When I woke up, I called my prayer partner, Deanne, whom I prayed with every morning before going to work. As I relayed the dream to her, which was still crystal clear in my mind, I heard myself say, "So I decided to quit and run out the back door." Upon hearing myself speak those words, I instantly remembered the prophetess telling me that I was trying to quit on something and run out the back door, but Jesus wouldn't let me and He was holding the door shut tight. At the same time, the Lord dropped in the revelation that the overwhelming thing that was too big for me to handle, was believing that without any dating involved, God was going to supernaturally identify my husband to me, identify me to my husband and bring us together to start preparing for marriage. I can't describe the love and thankfulness I felt towards the Lord when I realized that this was the reason that Jesus was holding the door shut tight! If it was my heart's desire to completely turn the husband-thing over to Jesus, He was even more determined than I, to see that it came to pass, by providing everything that was needed, and that included a gift of faith for me. With His faith in my heart, all unbelief concerning the Lord bringing my husband to me was permanently removed. As time went on, the faith He had put in my heart only grew stronger. Through His gift of the revelation from that dream, He had fully persuaded me that my God is even as His name – Faithful And True.

My Times Are In God's Hands

I had yet to learn the lesson that when we give a situation completely over to the Lord, that has to include the element of time. When I was only in the beginning of the wait for my husband, I knew that I had the faith to believe that God would bring my husband into my life by the time I turned 35. That meant that my husband would be coming sometime in the next year. As the months went by, I continued to believe and look forward to coming to the knowledge of who my husband was and having him brought into my life. When the time came close for my 35th birthday and there was no husband in sight, I realized with disappointment that it obviously wasn't going to happen within the time frame that I had believed. It was time to regroup! I knew that God couldn't fail me and I knew that I had truly stood in faith, but yet it hadn't happened. Why not? What God revealed to me when I asked for understanding was that I had tried to take control of a key element that has to be left in God's hands, and that is the timing. As I came to later realize, God does such a complete work, that many factors that we wouldn't even consider to be related to the issue are taken into account and put in order, so the finished work is all that He intends for it to be and nothing less!

For the vision is yet for an appointed time and it hastens to the end [fulfillment]; it will not deceive or disappoint. Though it tarry, wait [earnestly[for it, because it will surely come; it will not be behindhand on its appointed day.

Habakkuk 2:3

God Is My Encourager

During the time that I was on this fourteen-year faith journey, there were times, that I knew I needed some encouragement from the Lord – just something that would tell me, "Yes, I see you, I know what you are going through and even though you don't see anything happening with your natural eyes, be encouraged because your husband is real, he is alive and breathing, and it is still my plan to bring him to you." Every time that I asked for encouragement, within a matter of days something happened that kept my faith alive. God would give a message through the pastor that spoke exactly what I needed to hear, or a personal word would come through someone who knew nothing of my situation. God knew exactly what to do to supply me with His peace. God kept my faith tank filled before it ever hit empty.

NOW FAITH is the assurance (the confirmation, the title deed) of the things [we] hope for, being the proof of things [we] do not see *and* the conviction of their reality [faith perceiving as real fact what is not revealed to the senses].

Hebrews 11:1

God's faith in my heart and the encouragement that kept it strong, made my husband's existence just as real to me as though I could see and touch him. God is no respecter of persons; what He did for me, He will certainly do for you.

That is not to say, that at times I didn't feel the reproach of still being single when I was in my 30s and 40s. No one can say, "But you don't know what it's like to wait year after year or to see the years that you expected to be raising your children pass on by, or feel the reproach of being an old maid." I well understand all of those things and so does the Lord. Perhaps the most painful day of my wait was my 40th birthday, by which time I had hoped that my children would have all been brought into the world. God knows and cares about the desires of our hearts and He is a restorer. Some aspects about our lives we don't need to try to figure out. They need to be trustingly put in His hands.

And I will restore *or* replace for you the years that the locust has eaten—the hopping locust, the stripping locust, and the crawling locust, My great army which I sent among you.

And you shall eat in plenty and be satisfied and praise the name of the Lord, your God, Who has dealt wondrously with you, And my people shall never be put to shame.

Joel 2:25

God Is Well Able To Get Through To You!

One lie that the enemy speaks to the hearts of single people so they'll give up on the plan of God being their match-maker, is that they won't be able hear from God well enough to know when He is telling them that a particular person is their spouse. Rest assured, there is nothing so dense about you, that the God Who made you, and Who also made the universe is not capable of causing you to know what you need to know beyond a shadow of a doubt. As my story continues, you will see that when God began putting things in my knower to position me and identify my husband to me, I was just living my life, involved with every day activities, not even thinking anything about the husband-situation. I didn't happen to be in prayer or meditation, "trying to listen." Yes, God will speak to us during those times. But if you have released the match-making business into His hands, it is His responsibility to cause you to know what you need to know, and be where you need to be. So relax and enjoy the ride!

God knew that it needed to be settled in my heart that He would enable me to hear Him. Before I ever knew that God would do the match-making for me, I was at home, preparing to go back to school on a hot August day for Meet Your Teacher Night, and the Holy Spirit interrupted my thoughts and spoke loudly and clearly to my heart, that a particular man whom I knew, but had not seen or heard of for over a year was going to ask me for a date. God knew at the time that I wouldn't recognize that this was His voice, but He had a very clear purpose in mind for His communication to me. I paused and pondered on the information as though it were a fact, but then considered the thought my own and dismissed it. At eight o'clock that same evening that man called and asked me out. If I hadn't been so young in my experience with the Lord, I would have recognized that it was the Holy Spirit Who had spoken to me, and I would have asked Him what to do. His guidance could have saved me from "going around another mountain" that didn't bring me any closer to becoming a happily married woman. He knew that I wouldn't know His voice, but what He had spoken to me served a purpose for the future. He had demonstrated His ability to make me hear Him. As I matured in the Lord, I not only recognized that it was the Lord Who had spoken, but also that He had answered before I called on a need that I didn't yet have – the need to be fully persuaded that I could hear from Him about who my husband was. When the

Lord did impart information that I needed about my husband, He did it in a completely different manner, but because of that experience, the fear of my inability to hear was conquered.

Not Everyone Needs To Know

It isn't necessary or advisable to run around telling everyone you know that God is going to be your match-maker. Let's face it, to the world's thinking and even for most Christians, the idea that without any dating, God will identify you and your spouse to each other, fill your hearts with love, and bring you two together is pretty far-fetched. To save yourself the embarrassment of being thought of as a wacko or a flakey Christian, use wisdom in with whom you share this plan. The people who should know are mature Christians whom you know will keep your confidences private and will be able to stand in faith with you. Sometimes answers come quickly, and sometimes a wait for answers may be a number of years, as it was in my case. Imagine how silly I would have felt if I had broadcast to the masses my plan for getting a husband, and then ten years later nothing had happened. Abraham had a twenty-five year wait from the time the Lord promised Him that he would be a father of many nations, until the birth of Isaac, the son of the promise. We don't know if this promise was shared with any others, but I would imagine that for the most part that knowledge was hidden in the hearts of Abraham and Sarah and not common knowledge to all of their acquaintances.

I was blessed to have a number of Christian friends who were able to believe with me over the long haul. When the time came that their prayers for me were answered, it was a great blessing for them also, to see how the hand of God moved on my behalf. When a Christian man asked me for a date, I did share what I was believing God for, so I was able to say no without causing him to feel rejection. Over the years, there were also some close friends who cared enough to want to introduce me to single men that they thought might be a good match. Because of their thoughtfulness, although I knew they would think my plan for getting a husband was pretty unlikely to be successful, I did explain why I wasn't taking them up on their offer for help. When God did do what I had said He would do, it was a testimony to them of just how big He is.

Jesus Loves Me This I Know!

Every woman needs to know that she is deeply loved by the Lord. Be secure in the love He has for you and know that all of His promises in the Bible are for you. His Word is a love letter to you, His daughter. You were made to be a Daddy's girl. Thinking that God may not love you enough, or that you are not important enough to Him to choose your husband and bring him to you is believing a lie. It doesn't agree with what His Word says about His love for you. According to Psalm 17:8, you are the apple of His eye. That means you are His favorite! He rejoices over you with singing (Zephaniah 3:17). Song of Solomon reveals how intimately our Father loves us. In chapter 2:4 we are reminded that there is a protecting and comforting banner of love over our heads. God's love for you is unconditional. If there is sin in your life, repent and leave it in your past. His mercies are new for you every morning.

How precious *and* weighty also are Your thoughts to me, O God! How vast is the sum of them!
If I could count them, they would be more in number than the sand.
Psalm 139:17, 18a

Are not two little sparrows sold for a penny? And yet not one of them will fall to the ground without your Father's leave (consent) and notice.

But even the very hairs of your head are all numbered.

Fear not, then; you are of more value than many sparrows.

Matthew 10: 29-31

Behold, I have indelibly imprinted (tattooed a picture of) you on the palm of each of My hands; [O Zion] your walls are continually before Me.

Isaiah 49:16

A Prayer To Overcome Every Obstacle To Your Faith

Father, I ask that you would clothe and equip me to rest in You and wait in peace. You are my shield from confusion and fear. Lord, cause it to become big in my heart that You won't let me miss it. Thank you for your gift of faith. Thank you for encouraging me whenever I need it. I release to You the care of knowing what I need to know when I need to know it. I'm putting this in Your hands. Thank you for spiritual ears that hear and recognize You, and for spiritual eyes that see as You see. Help me to keep this in Your hands. Help me to walk in the spirit and not try to do anything to bring this about in my flesh. Please root any foolishness out of my heart. Thank you for giving me wisdom in guarding my heart. Thank you for counseling me and guiding me with your eye. Father, let Your Word grow stronger in me every day as you prepare me to be a wife. I can do all things through Christ Who strengthens me and that includes trusting you on this faith journey. This is not something that I am able to do myself, so Lord, thank you for doing it in me and through me. All things are possible with You! In Jesus' name. Amen.

The steps of a [good] man are directed and established by the Lord when He delights in his way [and He busies Himself with his every step].

Psalm 37:23

Chapter 4

Being Positioned

God's thoughts towards us are constant and He desires to be as involved in our lives as we allow Him to be. As we draw near to Him, He draws near to us. As you will see in the unfolding of events as the Lord positioned me to meet my husband, no detail was left unattended by His provision.

Buy A House!

The first time that I had the experience of God "filling my knower" with some knowledge from Him, was when I returned to my apartment from spring break in 1999, with the realization that I was going to buy a house. In this instance, as with all others, having my knower filled meant that God had dropped a piece of information into my spirit that I knew was from the Lord, and was in my heart in a place where doubt had no access. I didn't actually experience the being informed part, as in getting an impression, or hearing a voice audibly or in my spirit, but it was going from not knowing something one second, to having been informed the next. As I've said before, a distinct part of having my knower filled was a complete peace that whatever I had been informed of was a done deal and I was just along for the ride. It was like watching a good movie, in which you have already been told about the happy ending by someone else who has already seen it, (which in this case was God) but you don't know how the happy ending is going to be brought about. I was surprised by this revelation about a house, as I had always assumed that my future husband and I would pool our money together to buy one. Buying a house wasn't happening as I had envisioned it, and that wouldn't be the last time that I found things not happening in the order that I had presumed. With God, expect the unexpected. He is full of suddenlies. In December of '99, God filled my knower that by Christmas of 2000, I would be settled in my new home. Along with the knowledge that I was moving, God had given me a great anticipation and desire to move, so by Christmas time I had emotionally and mentally moved on from living in my apartment. I had put up no decorations due to a lack of interest, and we celebrated Christmas in my brother's new condo, rather than my apartment that was usually decorated to the hilt.

In January of 2000, I enlisted the help of a realtor and began looking at homes in Springfield that fit my budget. I knew that I was looking for the home for my husband and I to live in, but also recognized that with no husband in sight, I'd have to keep that information to myself. It wasn't long before it became very apparent that there was a big gap between what I needed and wanted in a home, and what I could afford. Because it wasn't my decision to buy a house, but God's, this lack of funds wasn't the least bit troubling to me. I was all the more interested to see how the events would play out, since I knew the end of the episode was that I was going to have the house He had chosen, and the provision was already there.

Before ever beginning to house hunt, I sat down with Christian girl friends who were my frequent prayer partners, and we prayed and agreed that just as with my husband, God would go before me and choose our house and identify it to me. God would consider who my neighbors would be, and He would know which house wouldn't need repairs that I could not afford to make. These are important considerations that we who don't know the future are in the dark about. We had also prayed in the years before that whatever the people who presently owned our house did to it color wise, would be agreeable to my furnishings, so it would be move-in ready.

In January and February I was busy packing to move to a house I had only by faith. By the end of February, eighty boxes were packed and labeled as to what room in my future house they belonged in, and sitting in my now very crowded living room. After two months of looking at houses that didn't come close to my criteria, one of the teachers at school, who lived in Decatur, casually mentioned that I may want to look at homes in that town, as they were less expensive. With that comment, God dropped into my knower that I was moving to Decatur, a town that would move me another 15 minutes farther from my school, making it a little over a half an hour away. Being one who hates to travel on icy roads in winter, it would never have been my idea to add on to that daily drive, but again I was filled with peace. The first five friends I confided to that God was moving me to Decatur all had a negative comment to make about it. Not being impulsive by nature, but one who thinks things out very deliberately, I would have been rethinking the move had it been my idea. Not being ruffled by those comments was another confirmation to me that this wasn't me, but the Lord. Their words had no effect on me whatsoever because God had settled it in my heart that for me, this would be a place of blessing. The anticipation and desire to move there just continued to increase, though I had very little personal knowledge of the town. I had made shopping trips to their mall and had gone to some teacher institutes held at Millikin University, which has a very charming campus. Other than two married teachers from my school, I didn't know a soul who lived there. So I was blissfully marching into the unknown, with trust in the Lord that He knew what He was doing.

My realtor connected me with a realtor in Decatur. In March, when I made my first trip to look at some houses in the neighborhood closest to the highway I'd be taking to school, I realized that God had chosen an old, tree-filled neighborhood, full of charm and full of houses that met my criteria for a family home. It was right next to Millikin and the two Decatur teachers also lived there. The homes were easily within the range of what was affordable! I immediately fell in love with everything about the neighborhood. Now for God to identify our home! A few weeks later, I was shown a house that was everything I wanted, but there was nothing from God. I remember sitting in the living room with my realtor and my friend Judy, who had accompanied me to look at every house both in Springfield and Decatur. My realtor was feeling a little frustrated. This was obviously a house with everything that I wanted, but she wasn't getting much reaction from me.

"Well now Mary, just what is it that you want in a house?" she asked.

What I wanted of course, was for God to fill my knower with the assurance that this was the one that He had chosen for me, but I knew in my spirit that that would sound completely ridiculous to her, so I simply replied, "I'm not sure." It made me look a little silly, but made more sense to her than the truth would have. As I drove away, I commented to my friend Judy, that if this wasn't my house, then God was giving me a pretty amazing house because I thought that this house was amazing!

Six weeks went by. In the meantime, I continued looking at other homes. The housing market was doing quite well, and houses in Decatur were selling like hot cakes. On three different occasions, my realtor called me at school during the day, to say that a home I was scheduled to see that afternoon had already been sold. In mid-May, God dropped in my knower that the amazing house that I had seen back in March *was* my house. Why the six week wait? There were a number of issues there were important to me that God wanted to wrap up, put in order and add His provision to, so everything about it would be the greatest blessing that it could be. Timing was important. Although the house was in move-in condition, God had held it open. It was important to me that my mother and brother be a part of looking at the house and making the bid. My mother had just moved from our family home into a condo in Bloomington and wanted her business with that to be finished before making the trip to look at the house. That meant it would need to sit for another week! Although anxious to get the house, I knew that God would continue to hold it open.

At the end of May, my bid was accepted and by mid-June I would be the proud owner of my own home, a home that was in colors that went with my furnishings, just as I'd prayed. This, for me, was the answer to a long awaited dream. I had watched most of my friends move into nice family homes in their 20s, but unable to afford a home on my own with a teacher's salary and not having the desire to live in a house by myself, I had continued apartment living until I was forty-five years old, with the dream of that someday house in front of me. I knew it would happen, but there were times, as with the dream of a husband, that it felt as if it would always be in the future.

Just two weeks before the move, my beloved cat, Jasmine, passed away. She had been my constant companion for the last 15 years and it was a very painful loss. As I would walk up the stairs to my apartment each day afterward, I felt as though a blanket of grief was being dropped down over me. If the move had come earlier, she would have passed away in my new home, and being old and deaf, her adjustment to a new place would have been traumatic for both of us. God had spared us from that trauma. Being in a new place where I had no memories of her, greatly helped in the healing process, and gave me the fresh start that I needed. Another testimony of the beauty of God's timing!

Everything about the move was marked with tremendous blessing. The help of many friends made it a time of happy fellowship. And now, as the last deliveries of my appliances were made, I was looking forward to wandering from room to room in sheer amazement at what the Lord had given me. The move was finished on a Friday after a week of daily deliveries, including moving vans from Springfield and Bloomington, which included some furniture from our family home, a U-Haul and numerous car loads. Unknown to me, the city of Decatur had planned to close off my street beginning the next Monday after the move, for the following two weeks to resurface the road. Yet, another example of God's timing! My move would have been impossible without vehicle access to my house.

I knew that this whole thing had been God positioning me to be in the right place to meet my husband. This move was about destiny, part of a much bigger picture than just moving from an apartment to a house. Oh, God! Lead me deeper into this adventure!

The Right Church

Where should I go to church? I knew God certainly had a plan for what body of believers He wanted to connect me with. Decatur was full of churches and I knew nothing about any of them. Because I had moved to Decatur to meet my husband, it seemed that being in the right church could have to do with being in the right place at the right time. But, having been wrong when I had presumed that God would bring my husband before my 35th birthday, I determined not to assume anything again.

I asked the Lord to direct me to the church where He wanted me, but rather than not go anywhere until I knew, I began by visiting a church that had been recommended by my former pastors. It had a small congregation similar to what I had come from. Everything about this little church was perfectly acceptable, but there was nothing from the Lord that this was "the place." One month after moving from Decatur, I was driving back to visit my former church to hear a special speaker. On the way over, I asked the Lord to strongly direct my attention to the particular church where He wanted me to be. Twenty minutes later, walking up the sidewalk to my old church, was a lady with whom the Lord had given me a close spiritual connection. She actually wasn't an attender of that church, but she was going to hear the special speaker also. She was a woman of great faith, a spiritual mentor to many. I had never personally known anyone who had walked so closely with the Lord and experienced such miracles as she. So it was a divine appointment when I told her that God had moved me to Decatur and she said I should visit Maranatha Assembly of God, as it was like "heaven on earth." God sent the one person whose opinion I would value most to direct me to my church. The following Sunday, I visited what would become my next church home. I went once and knew that it was God's choice. It just felt right!

Finding My Place

Once at Maranatha Assembly of God, the Lord finished the positioning process. I had heard that there was a Sunday school class for singles, but having been single for the last forty-five years, I had no desire to be separated from everyone else because of my singleness. I just wanted to blend in with the "normal people." I told God that if He wanted me to be a part of that, He would really have to draw my attention to it in a big way. The next Sunday after church, I was invited to go out to lunch with some of the other church goers. Almost as soon as I arrived at the restaurant, a lady whom I did not know asked in a loud voice why I wasn't going to the singles Sunday school class. I took that boldly-made remark as drawing my attention to it in a big way and went the next Sunday.

The class was taught by a friendly widower named Mike, who was also in his 40s. Very soon after beginning the class, he talked about wanting to hold an evening singles Bible study twice a month. I had told the Lord that my home was His home and so offered to host the Bible study. The stage was now set. The positioning complete!

One more time the Lord filled my knower before He directly addressed the husband-issue. Christmas of 2000, when I was celebrating with my family in my new home, just as the Lord had said I would, He revealed that by the next Christmas of 2001 I would have another cat. That spring He added Sophie and her daughter Sadie to the family; what would seem an unimportant event to most was of great importance to me. A close friend and I had often said, the Lord considers so many details about our personalities and their personalities in matching us up with our cats, just think of how carefully He will consider all things in matching us up with our husbands. As I enjoyed the company of my two little buddies, I once again remembered those conversations about God's faithfulness and my curiosity increased as to what my husband would be like.

As December of 2001 neared, it had been a year and a half since the move to Decatur. I had settled into my church, made some good friends and continued to host the singles Bible study, but I had begun to feel a sadness at not seeing the desire of a husband fulfilled. Everything within me said that I wasn't supposed to be single, but yet I was. I cringed inside when I heard the word "Miss" in conjunction with my name. As a second grade teacher, I had to endure hearing that title repeatedly throughout the day. I had been pregnant with this dream for too long and felt way past ready to see it birthed into the present.

Christmas of 2001, the Lord dropped into my knower that by Christmas of 2002 my husband would be in my life! I didn't know if that meant we would be married by then, but I knew we would be in each other's lives and would know that God had chosen us for each other. That word was like water to someone who is dying of thirst. It was an unexpected stream in the desert! In one instant, God had revived me and restored my joy in waiting. I was strong again and ready to move forward to receive this answer to my prayers.

Hope deferred makes the heart sick, but when the desire is fulfilled, it is a tree of life.

Proverbs 13:12

Chapter 5

The Desire Fulfilled

Very early in 2002, I knew from the Lord, that I would be married by Christmas of that year; I just had no idea to whom! In confirmation of that promise, in March I attended some weekend meetings at our church with a prophetess, Sandy Powell, who had come up to Decatur from Tennessee. On Saturday afternoon, we were told that she and Anita Mason, the head of Women Mentoring Women, the local women's ministry responsible for bringing her there, would be used by the Lord to bring some prophetic words to the women that evening. I was the first one to be called up from the congregation for a word by Anita. As I stood with my hands stretched outward to my sides to receive, the prophetess found her attention drawn to the ring finger on my left hand.

She said, "I keep looking at your ring finger expecting to see a ring because I see you as married."

"I do too!" I quickly responded.

"Oh, we're calling things that be not as though they were!" she laughed.

"Yes, I am," I said very seriously. Anita and Sandy proceeded to tell me that it was now time for me to meet my husband and gave me some words about him. What a wonderful experience to have him spoken about as a reality! And sometime in the very near future, he would finally have a name, a face and a personality. I had often felt during my wait that he didn't live in Springfield but lived far away. How close I must be to finding out what had for so long been a mystery!

My Husband's Home Too!

In early spring, I thought it might be nice to change the beige walls of my bedroom to lavender. I went to Bed, Bath and Beyond in Bloomington, where my mother lived, to look for a lavender bedspread first, before picking out the paint color. Even before finding what I was looking for, the Lord reminded me that this was going to be my husband's bedroom too, and He impressed upon my heart that when that room was changed it needed to be after my husband and I had agreed on the changes together. Although I knew I needed to obey the Lord, I charged a beautiful lavender bedspread, exactly what I had been hoping to find, and took it to Decatur just to see how it looked. I already knew that this was only to satisfy my curiosity and that it would be going right back to the store. I later found that my husband doesn't especially care for purple, so I saved myself a lot of trouble by listening to the Lord.

It occurred to me sometime that spring that there was no place in my bedroom for any of my husband's clothes and belongings, so I started making room for him. I emptied out exactly half of the bedroom closet, half of the chest of drawers, dresser drawers and night table drawers. They would remain empty until my husband put his clothes away when he moved in after our wedding. To me, those now empty places were a reminder that my husband was soon to be there and the act of preparing the way for him made it seem all the more a reality.

The Mystery Revealed

The end of a school year is filled with so many extra jobs to get the report cards out, the end-of-year reports made, and the classroom ready to close down for summer. There is so much extra stress and things to attend to, that even though there may only be two weeks of school left, the end seems far away because of the endless amount of work involved. It was the day after the close of school. My work was finished, the school year was behind me, and an open stretch of summer days was ahead. It was Wednesday, June 5th of 2002 and it was also the day that the Lord dropped into my knower the identity of my husband. I knew! I knew who he was! I knew his name! I knew what he looked like! And much to my complete surprise it was someone already in my life! It was Joe Turek, who had been coming to the singles Bible study at my home for the last ten months. With that knowing from the Lord having been imparted to me, the love that a wife should have for her husband was also starting to come, the love that had been saved for my husband for the last fourteen years! I felt an excitement about the next time that I would see him *in two days* on Friday. One of my second graders was appearing in the outdoor summer theatre in Springfield and before I had known anything about Joe being my husband, I had invited Mike, Carol and Joe, all members of the singles Bible study, to accompany me. This was the *only time* that I ever asked any men in the singles group to do something outside of a scheduled singles church activity. In my mind, none of us had *any* romantic interest in each other whatsoever! I had just thought it might be nice for a group of us to go watch my student perform. Mike had remarked that they had seen very little of me that spring because my mother had been in the hospital and my weekends had been spent with her. I asked him to go with Carol and me. Joe and Mike were good friends so Joe was added to the group.

Up until this revelation that Joe was my husband, although Joe had been coming pretty regularly to the Bible study since the August before, it was as though the Lord had kept him hidden from me and I just wasn't as aware of him as I was of everyone else. I had been in his presence every Sunday and two Thursday evenings a month, but I hadn't really seen him. I found out later that he had thought I was ignoring him during those times. If God doesn't want you to know something until an appointed time, you are not going to know it! I had a good impression of Joe and thought that he was a nice person but knew relatively little about him. I didn't even know for sure what line of work he was in. I had never had a thought that Joe may be my husband and had felt nothing towards him in that respect. That had been very evident in our last conversation just the Sunday before at a cookie fellowship after the evening church service. Joe's job as a comptroller at a local business had been ended as a result of his company closing the plant the previous January. He was in the process of interviewing for jobs.

Joe had said to the group, "Pray that I don't get this job in Peoria because I don't want to move to Peoria." Not wanting to make another big change to an unknown community, Joe was hoping to either find employment in Decatur or move back home. (God had moved Joe to Decatur from St. Simon's Island, Georgia, six weeks after I had moved to Decatur in the summer of 2000. So he had come from over a thousand miles away. The impression that I'd had when living in Springfield that my husband was living far away had been from the Lord.)

Trying to be encouraging and knowing that Joe also wanted to get married, I said, "But Joe, your wife could be in Peoria!"

Joe, who already knew that I was his wife, couldn't have found that remark very encouraging! Here it was, only three days later, and I saw Joe through completely new eyes! I was thrilled at the thought that he was the one for me! As Joe walked up the sidewalk to my front door to go to the play, as he had done so many other times to attend the Bible study, my heart beat excitedly that he was so close. I was suddenly feeling an attraction for him that had been non-existent just the week before, and I couldn't wait to spend an evening with him. As it turned out, Mike was unable to come, so Joe, Carol and I went together. Every minute felt like an answered prayer, as I enjoyed the wonderful secret that my long awaited husband was sitting by my side. Although my knower was full, (I was fully persuaded in my spirit), my mind was reeling from the shock of having such a long awaited dream suddenly brought from the future into the present.

The next afternoon, I was sitting at my kitchen table and saying out loud, "Lord, if this isn't him, it's going to take me months to get over him!" That is how deeply the Lord had already emotionally attached me to my man. Hollywood cannot outdo the Lord, God Almighty! Marriage is God's idea, and all the blessings the Lord had planned for this love story that He had so carefully written were starting to be poured out! I was falling head-over-heels in love with the man of my dreams, and the years of reproach and hope deferred had melted away with the past! I finally had a mate! I was just on the brink of embarking on our life as a kingdom couple! My heart overflowed with songs of praise and thankfulness to the Lord! I knew unspeakable joy! And I knew without a doubt, that this man was well worth the wait!!! That gift of faith from the Lord, the substance of things hoped for, the evidence of things not seen (Hebrews 11:1) that had gotten me through the last fourteen years had served its divine purpose in bringing about the union of Mary and Joseph Turek.

The Lord had sustained me. When I had wanted to quit and run out the back door, Jesus wouldn't let me. He had been there the whole time, holding the door shut tight. I knew this was the beginning of many miracles and God-adventures that the Lord had planned for us on our journey through life. I was ready to set sail. Whatever lay ahead, Jesus would be there taking us through!

Adjusting To The New Normal

Imagine what it would be like after years of serious financial struggles, to learn that you had won the lottery and would be receiving large sums of money on a regular basis for years to come. Life as you knew it would never be the same because of the blessing that had been dropped into your life! This is the kind of a change that had burst into my life on June 5th, 2002. Yes, I had known it would happen, but when a lifetime desire is met after fourteen years of living with it in the future, you can't stop pinching yourself that it has actually happened. One reason the Lord had waited until school was out to bring the breakthrough, was so I would have the time to be consumed with it, to revel in it, to ponder it, to rejoice in it. Words cannot describe how sweet is the time and how triumphant is the feel of a long awaited answered prayer.

When talking about the revelation of Joe being my husband with a friend who had supported me in faith over the years, I realized that the Lord had literally brought my husband to my door step by bringing him week after week to the singles Bible study. The reason God had done it that way was because people had said that He wouldn't! Well-meaning people in my life had believed that Mary needs to get out there, meet people and date. The Lord was revealing Himself to them as the Faithful One With No Limits. Later, when the new school year started, and Joe and I were engaged, one of the retired teachers who had heard through the grapevine some of the details of what God had done, came to school to congratulate me. She said that she and another retired teacher would get on the phone and just laugh with amazement that God had done everything that I had believed He was going to do.

Waiting For My Husband To Pursue Me

Having my husband identified to me was only the beginning of the Lord putting us together and I wanted to be careful not to get in His way and do anything to hinder Him. God was going to do the whole thing or it wasn't going to happen; that was my stance. That meant it was up to Joe to hear from God to know that it was time to pursue me. He had to hear from God, not from me. I couldn't go tell him that I knew he was my husband although I could tell from the attention he gave me that he knew I was his wife and that was good news to him! As the husband, Joe was the head and I had to let him lead.

All through June and July, the Lord put Joe and I together every few days, but with other people present. We helped someone move, or we attended a singles function. God put us together unusually often. One day our group went to Abraham Lincoln's New Salem, just west of Springfield. As Joe stood closely behind me and we watched a re-enactment of a pioneer wedding, I wondered if Joe was thinking as I was, that we too would soon be standing before our friends and exchanging wedding vows. God orchestrated these times together so Joe had the opportunity to see the great change in my behavior towards him. I was no longer oblivious to his presence but went straight to him to sit close by his side. He needed to know for sure that it was time to come forward. That would take some courage because everyone in the Bible study knew about my rule of not spending time with any man alone until God had identified him to me as my husband. Joe needed that confirmation that the Lord had finally revealed to me that he was my husband. Joe had known God had chosen me for him since early spring when the Lord started speaking to his heart to get to know Mary.

At the end of July, the singles had a breakfast in a large pavilion in the park near my home. Everyone gradually went home until Joe and I were the only two left.

45

It was then that Joe asked, "Can we start spending some time alone together?" I knew that he knew in asking that question, he was saying, "Do you know that I am your husband?"

He was visibly relieved when I answered, "Yes!"

Right then he put his head down and whispered, "Thank you Jesus."

We both knew that we both knew what God was doing!

A few days later when driving to church on Wednesday evening, God let me know that it was time to respond to Joe's lead, by sharing my side of the match-making experience, so I asked him to come over after church. I told him how and when the Lord had shown me that we were husband and wife. That Sunday morning, I walked with Joe up to our pastor who was standing in the hall.

Joe said to him, "I have two words for you – marry us!"

"Really? I'd love to!" was Pastor Doug's response. I felt it was the Lord's blessing that there was no hesitation, no question in our pastor's mind that this was a good idea, even though he hadn't seen us spending the time together that would be natural for two people who are moving towards marriage. But this engagement wasn't natural. It was supernatural. We had been supernaturally paired up as husband and wife. God Himself was joining us together!

Betrothed!

We both knew deep in our spirits and discussed this knowing that before the foundation of the world, it had been God's plan to put us together as husband and wife. Joe felt that because of God having put us together, we were betrothed and not just engaged. What was the difference? Mary and Joseph in the Bible were betrothed. A period of betrothal preceded Jewish marriages at that time. Betrothal was more than engagement. Except for actual cohabitation, betrothal was considered to be a legal marriage in every other way. The man could not renounce the woman except by divorce, and if he died, she was considered a widow. The two usually did not know each other before the betrothal as the marriage was arranged by their parents. Our marriage had been arranged by our Heavenly Father. Betrothal lasted for a year. Then after the marriage ceremony, the couple began living together as husband and wife. Joe and I were betrothed for a little less than four months before we were married. When we had been spending time together for only a few weeks, Joe commented that the Lord had made it seem as though we had spent months together. I noticed it too. God had taken us out of our time zone and brought us into His. We had been given a gift of time!

Gold Dust - A Sign Of God's Glory

Just weeks after our engagement, which began when Joe and I had openly acknowledged to each other that we knew the Lord had chosen us to be husband and wife, we started working on a wedding date. By the first of September, the date was set for December 21, 2002. Just as God had dropped in my knower, I would be married that year!

In September, the same women's ministry that had brought Sandy Powell, the prophetess, up from Tennessee was holding a women's weekend retreat, and Sandy had returned to minister. She asked if I would be willing to share my testimony about God being my match-maker to the eighty women who were in attendance. When I sat down after speaking, the woman sitting next to me noticed that I had gold particles all over my face and asked me what it was. I had no idea what she was talking about, and then I saw that I had what looked like gold glitter from a Hallmark card all over my clothes. Sandy said gold dust had appeared on her Bible and other places, a number of times when she had been ministering. It was a sign of God's glory. The gold dust on my face and clothes was a sign that confirmed that the testimony I had given was of the Lord, and it had been His work that was putting Joe and me together as husband and wife. Curious as to how I looked, I went into the restroom to look in the mirror. *Sparkly gold dust was all over my face!* About an hour later, it gradually disappeared. For months afterwards, one of the gals that had been at the meeting referred to me as the gold dust girl. If anyone had questioned the authenticity of my story about God being my match-maker and thought that I had finally just gotten lucky, God had removed that deception. God verified the words of my testimony with a supernatural sign that could not have happened without Him.

God had done it all! He had supernaturally shown Joe that I was his wife and shown me that he was my husband. He had supernaturally planted in both of us all the love, attraction, and romantic feelings that a husband and wife would want to feel for each other. We couldn't wait to get married, and we wanted to shout to the world that we were engaged. Joe and I had never dated. God had arranged meeting after meeting, without any planning or communication between us, up until the time that we both knew the Lord had chosen us for each other and we had openly acknowledged it. As we began our engagement, fully committed to each other, the Lord used the time spent together to develop the emotional intimacy that prepared us for marriage. Joe and I hadn't picked each other, but we couldn't have been happier with God's choice.

Those Christian friends who had stood with me over the years, believing that the Lord would send my husband, didn't need a sign to know that this union was of the Lord. Seeing their prayers for me answered was a great blessing to them as well. Precious friends that the Lord had placed in my life cried tears of joy at what God had done. How beautiful is the body of Christ!

A Three Stranded Cord Is Not Quickly Broken

Two friends in particular had prayed steadfastly with and for me about the Lord bringing my husband into my life. In December of 2001, the Lord had given me the scripture that we were as a three stranded cord that He had put together. Early summer of 2002, God spoke to my heart that He was making me a part of a new three stranded cord with Joe. The Lord Himself was the third strand that would be holding us together throughout our marriage. The words I had inscribed inside Joe's wedding band are " Ecc. 4:12 Joe Jesus Mary." I put Jesus' name between Joe's and mine because He needs to be in the center of our lives, our marriage and all that we do.

And though a man might prevail against him who is alone, two will withstand him. A threefold cord is not quickly broken.

Ecclesiastes 4:12

Every kingdom couple should be part of a three stranded cord with their spouse and the Lord. Even some God ordained marriages have failed. We need Christ-centered lives in order to withstand the attacks of the enemy and to fulfill our God-given purpose.

I Sing For Joy At The Work Of Your Hands!

Our wedding day was clothed in prayer. God's blessings were in every detail. Four days before Christmas, our church guests arrived under sunny blue skies on dry pavement.

Ordinarily an emotional person, I floated through the day with a calm joy. God's presence was there with us and the atmosphere in the sanctuary, as our family and friends gathered for the ceremony, was one of great celebration.

Joe, who had also not been previously married, had wanted *The Wedding Song,* to be a part of his wedding for years. It had very often been a part of weddings back in the 70s, when most of our peers had been married. With words that acknowledged the Lord's presence, and scripture that declares that the marriage union is God's plan, *The Wedding Song* set the stage, and our wedding ceremony began. Joe took his place at the front of the sanctuary ready to be united with me in marriage.

Standing in the church foyer in my wedding dress, with my brother Bob, I was prepared to walk down the aisle to become Mrs. Joseph Turek. With one hand holding my bridal bouquet of cascading roses, and the other raised to the Lord, I once again worshiped with all my heart as the soloist sang *Shout To The Lord* before the congregation. For years, whenever I sang the words *I sing for joy at the work of your hands,* I had looked to the day that would begin a union that was the work of His hands. I had declared numerous times that this song had to be sung at my wedding.

God also met another desire of my heart that day. Five years before, realizing my father was soon going to be with the Lord, I cried out to God in desperation and faith, that my dad wasn't going to be there to see me get married and I needed for Him to do something about it to make it ok. Within a tenth of a second, the scripture "we are now surrounded by so great a cloud of witnesses" came to my mind and I knew that was God's promise that my dad would still see it. My brother later confided that as we had worshipped in the foyer, and he had stood in my dad's place, ready to give me away, he had almost been brought to tears because of feeling my dad's presence, a sweet confirmation from the Lord, that He had fulfilled His promise.

God Knew That I Needed You was sung during our ceremony. It began with words that seemed to be written just for us, *"I look at you and I see the one God chose for me."* Although our eighth anniversary has passed, I still sometimes marvel that I have a husband, and that he is such a perfect match. God considered every detail of our personalities in putting us together. Joe and I have a broad range of gifts and abilities with few in common. We are much greater, more equipped to meet life's challenges and stronger together than we ever were alone. The three stranded cord has brought strength and peace to our lives. It has kept us in unity and kept us in love.

This is a story of God's faithfulness that is still being written. We have desires and dreams birthed in our hearts by the Lord that are yet to be fulfilled, but they will be in their appointed time! God has filled my knower with the substance of these things hoped for, and this knowing *is the evidence* of what is not yet seen.

Delight yourself also in the Lord, and He will give you the desires *and* secret petitions of your heart.
Psalm 37:4

Commit your way to the Lord [roll and repose each care of your load on Him]; trust (lean on, rely on, and be confident) also in Him and He will bring it to pass.

Psalm 37:5

Chapter 6

Taking Your Own Leap Of Faith

Keeping Focused On The Lord

God has plans not only for your future, but He also has plans and purposes for the present. One of the key ways that Satan takes singles off God's plan for their lives is by causing them to be distracted and busy with the business of finding a mate. His aim is to burden you with the false responsibility of being your own match-maker and to keep you from focusing on what God would really have you set your hands to. He wants to take you off the course the Lord would have you to be on, by robbing you of your peace and bringing confusion about where your focus should be. When you have released the husband-situation to the Lord and made Him your match-maker, you are free to better focus on Him so He can lead, guide and direct you. It is the enemy's lie that we can't be happy until we are married, or that we won't really start living our lives until that happens. Although one of the deepest desires of my heart was to be married and have a family, in the years that I was waiting the Lord provided me with a teaching career that was deeply fulfilling and brought friendships into my life that have turned into life-long God-connections. He surrounded me with encouragers that He used to speak life and strength into my heart when I needed to hear it, and He caused me to grow strong in Him. God used that time to reveal to me that He, not my husband, is my source for what I need. Although my husband makes me happy and I enjoy the blessings of our life together, I know that the Lord is my source for joy and everything else I need and want. God has chosen to use my husband to bring some blessings into my life, but God can bring joy and satisfaction into my life in any way that He chooses. Don't put God in a box or limit Him by thinking He should do things in a certain way. He knows the desires of your heart and He knows best how and when to bring them about. God will not make you wait longer than what is necessary and He will not forget what you have put in His hands. God promises us in His Word that as we put Him first, He will provide for all of these other things that He knows we have need of. Your life is not on hold until you get married, and your peace and enjoyment of life is not on hold either.

Therefore do not worry *and* be anxious, saying, What are we going to have to eat? or What are we going to have to drink? or,What are we going to have to wear?

For the Gentiles (heathen) wish for *and* crave and diligently seek all these things, and your heavenly Father knows well that you need them all.

But seek (aim at and strive after) first of all His kingdom and His righteousness (His way of doing and being right), and then all these things taken together will be given you besides.

So do not worry *or* be anxious about tomorrow, for tomorrow will have worries *and* anxieties of its own. Sufficient for each day is its own trouble.

Matthew 6:31-34

God is saying don't worry! Don't fret, wondering, "Who am I to marry? When is it going to happen? How am I going to know who it is? What if I miss it? Does God realize how old I am? Where is he? Why isn't he here yet?" Every concern that we have is to be placed in God's hands so He can care for us. The Lord wants us to completely rely on, depend on and trust Him for all things and see Him as the answer for all of our needs and the source of our supply.

> **Every good gift and every perfect (free, large, full) gift is from above; ...**
>
> **James 1:17a**

> **Lean on, trust in, *and* be confident in the Lord with all your heart *and* mind and do not rely on your own insight *or* understanding.**
> **In all your ways know, recognize, *and* acknowledge Him, and He will direct *and* make straight *and* plain your paths.**
>
> **Proverbs 3:5, 6**

> **Casting the whole of your care [all your anxieties, all your worries, all your concerns, once and for all] on Him, for He cares for you affectionately *and* cares about you watchfully.**
>
> **1 Peter 5:7**

God has a purpose for this present season of your life. The Lord has a plan for you today, and He will use the events and situations in this season to prepare you for what He has for you to do in the future. When I was single, two factors helped me to develop a solid prayer life that caused the Word of God to take deep root. First, God brought women prayer partners into my life whom I prayed with regularly. He also brought some prayer materials to my attention that were prayers over many subjects all compiled from scripture. Every morning for more than five years I prayed on the phone before I went to work with my prayer partner, Deanne. We often used the book *Prayers That Avail Much: An Intercessor's Handbook of Scriptural Prayers* from Word Ministries, Inc. Every day we prayed for our church, our country, our own situations and for people God had put upon our hearts. God started developing my inner library of scriptures through those daily prayer confessions as one of us read/prayed aloud and the other silently agreed. We interceded for every situation the Lord brought to our attention. Even today when I read the Word, I automatically watch for new scriptures to pray and declare over myself and others. God continues to add on to that library so the Holy Spirit can easily bring the appropriate scriptures to mind as I pray alone or as I minister. Another prayer partner, Sally, and I got together to pray on Thursday evenings for several years beginning at 7:30 pm. Watching *The Cosby Show* first at 7:00 was an absolute must! Then it was time for prayer. We usually spent several hours praying and agreeing together over every detail that came to mind for a given need.

He also assigned me to teach children's church, a very time consuming job that took hours of preparation, as I sought His face for the lessons, skits and spiritual principles that He wanted me to impart. God used this experience to develop in me an understanding of spiritual principles that prepared me to walk victoriously through some trials He knew would be in my future. God doesn't waste His time or our time either. There were divine purposes for that season in my life although I couldn't see what they were, other than to equip the children. I had no idea just how much He was equipping me for the future. Had I been focused on getting out there to meet my husband, I would have been distracted from the tasks at hand, and God couldn't have accomplished in my life what He did. I remember having the thought that I was so busy between teaching children's church and teaching my first graders at the elementary school, that even if God had brought my husband into my life, I didn't have time to have a relationship with him.

I think that thought was the Lord's way of speaking to my heart that the time is not yet, but it is still to come.

His promise in Romans 8:28 is that all things will work for our good because we love Him. The time that you are waiting for your husband will work for your good and will be to your advantage. The Lord is also working in your husband's life to prepare him for you and for your lives together. Take some time to pray for yourself and your husband that God's preparation is being accomplished in both of your lives and you are being perfected for each other and your kingdom couple destinies.

Enjoy and appreciate *this* season. Do not get in the mindset that life will begin when you get married. Have fun with the people God has put in your life for this time. Be deliberate about developing strong friendships with other Christian women. They will be a great support system. Some of those relationships may last a life time. Live in the present!

> **To everything there is a season, and a time for every matter *or* purpose under heaven:**
> **A time to be born and a time to die, a time to plant and a time to pluck up what is planted.**
> **A time to kill and a time to heal, a time to break down and a time to build up.**
> **A time to weep and a time to laugh, a time to mourn and a time to dance.**
> **A time to cast away stones and a time to gather stones together.**
> **A time to embrace and a time to refrain from embracing.**
> **A time to get and a time to lose, a time to keep and a time to cast away.**
> **A time to rend and a time to sew, a time to keep silence and a time to speak.**
> **A time to love and a time to hate, a time for war and a time for peace.**
>
> **Ecclesiastes 3:1-8**

My frame was not hidden from You when I was being formed in secret [and] intricately *and* curiously wrought [as if embroidered with various colors] in the depths of the earth [a region of darkness and mystery].

Your eyes saw my unformed substance, and in Your book all the days (of my life) were written before ever they took shape, when as yet there was none of them.

Psalm 139: 15, 16

As you commit your way to the Lord, He will cause you to step into His timing and you and your husband will be brought together in His appointed time. Until then, let Him continue to do His perfect work in your life. Some women may need healing from the past for things that have caused trauma or wounds in their hearts before they are ready to begin their lives with their husbands. When we are crippled emotionally, we don't function as well in our relationships. God knows what you've been through and what process to bring you through for complete healing. He will orchestrate what needs to be done so when He brings you and your husband together, you will be ready to be the wife that He created you to be. He will consider all things so it will be the great blessing in every way that He intends, and you won't be robbed because a few circumstances weren't quite in place.

Yet, O Lord, You are our Father; we are the clay, and You are our Potter, and we all are the work of Your hand.

Isaiah 64:8

Search me [thoroughly], O God, and know my heart! Try me and know my thoughts!

And see if there is any wicked *or* hurtful way in me, and lead me in the way everlasting.

Psalm 139:23, 24

In the meantime, God is your husband. He wants to be the lover of your soul. You are waiting for your earthly husband, but as a part of the body of Christ, you were created to be Christ's bride and He cherishes you.

You are whole in Him; you are not waiting to be made whole when you are united to your husband. The Word says, "And the two shall become one." It doesn't say, " And the two halves shall become one." Let Jesus be your first love and everything else will fall into place.

A Prayer To Stay Focused On Him

Father, thank you for the purposes that you have for me today and in this season that I am waiting for you to bring my husband. Lord, please cleanse my heart from anything that would hinder Your perfect work in my life. Thank you for preparing my husband and me for each other and for the lives that we will have together. Help us both to live in the present with you. Help us to have an attitude of gratitude, so our hearts are receptive and responsive to the work of your Holy Spirit. Lord, make me teachable and keep my ears open to your voice. Lord, heal my heart from the past and set me free to be whole in You. You are my source for everything I need and want. Establish your priorities in my life and fill my heart with your desires. Thank you for your focus, peace, direction, protection and provision. In Jesus' name.

Advantages To Having A God Chosen Husband

Trials come. It's a part of life. The enemy is as a roaring lion, looking for whom he may devour. When you know that your marriage union is God's doing, the enemy will never be able to convincingly whisper in your ear that you made a mistake, that you missed it. It is forever settled in your heart that marrying this man was God's perfect will. It will keep you in a victory mindset. You'll have an expectation for full recovery whatever comes, and the dream of walking in the fullness of your full destiny as a kingdom couple won't be shaken because of a few high waves or strong winds.

God has a plan for your life. There are things for you to accomplish in His kingdom. There are divine purposes that He wants to bring forth through you, and through you and your husband as a kingdom couple. Do you have the ability to know your full destiny or someone else's? Could you possibly know how God would want to blend your gifts to work together? Can you see into another person's heart to know what is really there? Of course you can't, but God knows and considers the answers to all of these questions. Is who you become one with important in terms of fulfilling the plans and purposes God has for your life? I would say it is hugely important! That being the case, would you want to blindly pick someone on your own or allow your Heavenly Father to bring the one that He would choose? He knows the desires of your heart. He knows what will bring the most blessing into your life and He wants you, His beloved daughter to trust, rely on and completely depend on Him for everything.

If you are reading this and you know that you chose your mate and not the Lord, know that He wants for you also to have a blessed marriage! Release your marriage and your life to Him. Trust Him to align you with His good plans and purposes. He loves you and wants you to experience the fullness of His blessings.

For I know the thoughts *and* plans that I have for you, says the Lord, thoughts *and* plans for welfare and peace and not for evil, to give you hope in your final outcome.
Jeremiah 29:11

I [the Lord] will instruct you and teach you in the way you should go; I will counsel you with my eye upon you.
Psalm 32:8

When you are peacefully waiting for the Lord to bring your husband to you, you are also safe from experiencing trauma and hurt from becoming involved with the wrong person and going through a painful break-up. Your heart is protected! A whole person without a lot of baggage from broken relationships is in a much better condition to function well in a healthy marriage. God has to heal us when our hearts are broken, and trauma from the past can distort our perceptions and wreak havoc in relationships. It is much better to avoid situations that God never intended for us to be in, than for Him to have to clean up the mess and take us through a healing process. But if a healing process is what you need, He can and will heal your wounds and make you whole again.

Honoring God

Our society as a whole, has embraced the idea of the couple living together as husband and wife before the marriage. It is accepted and considered to be normal, even expected. But God doesn't change. Jesus is the same today, yesterday and forever, and His Word is eternal and unchanging. The marriage bed is undefiled, but God makes it clear in His Word that sex outside of marriage is sin against your own body. Since the wages of sin is death, the enemy of our souls wants to bring as many as possible to participate in activity that opens the door for him to come in and steal, kill and destroy. Keeping sex within the boundary of marriage keeps you under God's protection. As Christians, we are to be holy, as God is holy. It is God's grace at work in us, that empowers a couple that is so head-over-heels in love, to wait until marriage to bring sexual intimacy into their relationship. When you know that you are the Lord's and your marriage is in existence because it was first His plan and brought about through His work, you will really have a revelation that marriage is holy! There was such gratefulness and recognition in our hearts that our union was the work of His hands, we did not want to dishonor and hurt the Lord by not being obedient to His Word in respect to our behavior towards each other.

When we receive Jesus as our Lord and savior, His grace is imparted to us. His grace anoints and equips us to live our lives in obedience to His Word and glorify Him. His mercies are new every morning because He knows that we don't always walk in the grace that has been freely given us. God's rules are given in love to shield us from the consequences the enemy would bring into our lives because of our ignorance. God said, "My people perish for lack of knowledge." Satan's lie is that if two people love each other, then sex before marriage is ok because God is merciful and He will be willing to overlook it. That is a deception. Obedience to God's Word will protect us from the landmines the enemy has set before us. Just as landmines are hidden, because of lack of revelation of God and His Word, for many Christians the truth that there are consequences to this sin has also been hidden. Sin opens the door to the enemy! When we walk out from under the protection that comes from obedience to God's Word, we have given the enemy permission to rob us in some area.

If you are reading this and realize that you were or are in this sin, or any other kind of sin, the good news is that God will wipe your slate clean. Jesus paid the great price with His life for your freedom from sin. Ask God to forgive you and ask Him to cleanse your heart and multiply His grace in your life so you can stay free. As far as the east is from the west, God has promised that our sin is as far from us when we repent and turn away from it. Because of His love for us, God has chosen to place that sin in the sea of forgetfulness as though it never existed (Micah 7:19). There is now no condemnation for those who are in Christ Jesus! We don't have to carry guilt (Romans 8:1).

A Prayer To Make God Your Match-Maker

Father, I'm asking you to be my match-maker. I release the whole husband-situation to you; it's in your hands now! Thank you for the grace to do this in You. I can't do it myself. My times are in your hands. My life is in your hands. Protect my heart! Protect my mind from confusion and cause me to walk in your peace. Thank you for preparing my husband and me for our lives together. Thank you for causing us to be in the right place at the right time because You order our steps. Father, align me and the one that you have chosen for me in our hearts, our minds, our emotions, our wills and our circumstances with Your will. Thank you for filling my knower and my husband's knower in your appointed time with all that we need to know, so You can complete the work of bringing about this union that you have planned. And Lord, help us to walk in your grace so our relationship remains pure and pleasing to you throughout our courtship. Thank you for a marriage that is blessed of the Lord. I will give you all the honor and the glory! In Jesus' name! Amen.

And this is the confidence (the assurance, the privilege of boldness) which we have in Him: [we are sure] that if we ask anything (make any request) according to His will (in agreement with His own plan), He listens to *and* hears us.

And if (since) we [positively] know that He listens to us in whatever we ask, we also know [with settled and absolute knowledge] that we have [granted us as our present possessions)] the requests made of Him.

1 John 5:14, 15

Part 2

What About My Husband, Lord?

Encouragement and Wisdom
For The Married Woman

Introduction

What About My Husband, Lord?

Encouragement and Wisdom
For The Married Woman

When a married woman turns to the Lord with the question – *"What about my husband?"* - it is because she is seeing some things that make it appear that her husband is not going in the direction of victory. As married women, we have a key role in helping our husbands to walk victoriously into their full destinies. Through the light of God's Word, the Lord gives us revelation as to what that role is.

The enemy wants us to carry the burden of trying to "fix" our husbands because he is hoping to use our behavior to bring devastation to our marriage relationship. God's Word is our GPS system. He will recalculate our route and direct us back on the pathway of life with His Word.

God brought the word *landmine* to my attention as He ministered to me through this message. A landmine is planted by the enemy for the purpose of bringing severe injury and death. The location of the landmine looks like a safe place so an unsuspecting person will step right on top of it, thinking it will be alright to walk there. God reveals the locations of the landmines through His Word. In other words, His Word gives us wisdom and direction so we know what to do and *what not to do*. God wants to equip us to be successful and blessed in our marriages and to be blessings to our husbands.

If we remain ignorant of God's Word, we'll do what makes sense to our natural minds, get off God's path, and unknowingly step on one of those marriage relationship landmines planted by the enemy. God means for us to walk in peace before we see the victory with our natural eyes, and let Him do His perfect work. God knows exactly what to do and how to do it. This is about allowing your Heavenly Father to carry the burden of doing His perfect work in your husband and freeing you to be the woman He has called you to be!

Let be and be still, and know (recognize and understand) that I am God.

Psalm 46:10a

Chapter 1

You Are His Cheerleader. God Is His Coach!

What do you do when you think that your husband is making choices that will not take him in the direction of victory and you think that what he needs to do is fairly obvious? If you are like most women, especially because you know that you are meant to be your husband's helpmate, it makes the most sense to your natural mind to help him by simply pointing out what he really should be doing. This is a landmine carefully planted by the enemy of our souls, and we step on it thinking it is the right way to go because it deceptively appears safe. In this chapter we are going to begin looking at what the Lord has to say about this in 1 Peter 3:1. The Lord knew this would be a sensitive issue, and also an issue that could come up on a daily basis, so special care and attention has been given to address it. He has given us specific instructions to order us away from this very innocent looking landmine. God's Word is that GPS system that will recalculate our route and get us back on the right track!

In like manner, you married women, be submissive to your own husbands [subordinate yourselves as being secondary to and dependent on them, and adapt yourselves to them], so that even if any do not obey the Word [of God],

they may be won over not by discussion but by the [godly] lives of their wives.

1 Peter 3:1

God's Word is His will and it's our instruction book of victory. To paraphrase 1 Peter 3, when your husband is not aligned in some way in his heart and his mind with the Word, and therefore is not walking in it, which means he is not going in the direction of victory in that area, he will not be convinced to change by the coaching of his wife. *Not by discussion!* Apparently, God has a better way! But it's one thing to keep your mouth closed when someone in a distant canoe is choosing to paddle in a way that keeps him going in circles, and another to keep your mouth shut when you are in the same boat with him! Because you and your husband are one, it would seem that you should be explaining about the better way to paddle that will get you where you want to go. This is one of those times that what seems right to our natural minds isn't going to get us the results that we are hoping for. Because our lives are so entwined with our husbands' and what affects them affects us, the enemy applies pressure through fear of what might happen if we don't speak up, to push us right into his landmine!

There is a way which seems right to a man *and* appears straight before him, but at the end of it is the way of death.

Proverbs 14:12

God reminds us in Romans 8:7 that our carnal minds are hostile to God. That means that sometimes, because we are lacking in complete understanding, we don't always come to the right conclusion. But God has promised to lead us around the landmines of the enemy! And that is just what He is doing in 1 Peter 3.

I [the Lord] will instruct you in the way you should go;
I will counsel you with my eye upon you.

Psalm 32:8

The Holy Spirit began ministering to me on this subject shortly after a board meeting for Guiding Light Ministries Healing Rooms in which our director said that the Lord was showing him that we were to hold a Saturday morning women's service. God had already told him that the name of the message was *What About My Husband, Lord?* And then he looked at us three ladies sitting around the table, and announced that one of us would be giving the message. Within a day or two, the Lord started ministering His wisdom on this subject to me, which came at a time when I was greatly in need of it. As I shared this life giving word with my friends, their reactions confirmed that this had been a landmine that they had walked through repeatedly. The only women seemingly not needing this instruction were those already familiar with the Lord's counsel in 1 Peter 3.

As the Lord was teaching me on this subject, an audio version of [2]*Wild At Heart* by John Eldredge made its way into my hands. This had been a book used for a men's Sunday school class at our church, and as I listened to one of the CDs, the Lord began opening up my understanding about the wisdom of verse 1 in 1 Peter 3. John Eldredge was explaining that in the heart of every man there is a desire for three things: a battle to fight, an adventure to live, and a beauty to rescue. If none of these attributes are visible in a man, it is because he no longer has the confidence to believe that he can accomplish these desires.

Christians must have confidence to walk in their full God-destinies. We need to have confidence in the skills and abilities that God has given us. Not every Christian will walk in his or her full destiny, but those who answer the call to come out into the deep with Him will need to have complete confidence that through the Lord, they will be enabled to operate beyond the natural abilities that they have been given. As a wife, you play an important role in building your husband's confidence, which he will need to walk in the plans and purposes the Lord has for him individually, and with you as a kingdom couple. Because of the role that you play in his life, you are not the messenger that God would use to coach him. *God is his coach and you are his cheerleader!*

When we leave our role as encourager/cheerleader and slide into the coach position, we are being counter-productive in our marriage relationship We can unknowingly be chipping away at our husbands' confidence that they need to walk in victory. Life is out of God's order so good can't come from it. By getting in God's way and trying to take over His role as coach, we can actually slow down the process that the Lord is taking our husbands through to bring victory into their lives. The result is that we are tearing down rather than building up. As we painstakingly advise our husbands, we are driving on the wrong highway, speeding along in a direction that will never get us to our desired destination!

God's promise that He will instruct, counsel and guide applies to your husband too. The Lord may give him visions and dreams. He may move in a situation that your husband is in to reveal what he needs to see. He may speak directly to his heart or He may use pastors, counselors or prophets to speak into his life and some of these people may be women. Your womanhood is not the reason that the Lord is not using you to counsel your husband in the right way to go. It is because of the special role that you have as his wife. You are the encourager/cheerleader! Your husband won't be able to see you as his encourager and cheerleader, which he so desperately needs, when you are trying to be his coach at the same time. Don't underestimate the importance of your true role. Vital to a healthy marriage is your husband's assurance that he has your support as his personal cheerleader!

Your word is a lamp to my feet and a light for my path.

Psalm 119:105

Chapter 2

Honoring Your Husband

The Lord is counseling us as wives, on *how* to build our husband's confidence and excel in our role as their encourager and cheerleader in verse 2 of 1 Peter 3.

When they observe the pure *and* modest way in which you conduct yourselves, together with your reverence [for your husband; you are to feel for him all that reverence includes: to respect, defer to, revere him—to honor, esteem, appreciate, prize, and, in the human sense, to adore him, that is, to admire, praise, be devoted to, deeply love and enjoy your husband].

1 Peter 3:2

Even the world recognizes the importance of the wife's support for her husband. "Behind every good man is a good woman" is the well-known expression that shows understanding of a man's need for his wife's support. He needs to know that she believes he is up to the challenge of being successful in his pursuits. In every woman's heart is the desire for her husband to be able to handle the pressures and responsibilities of being the head of his home, being a good husband and father, and being successful in the work place. As Christian women we all long to see our husbands boldly take their position as the spiritual head,

73

who encourage us as their wives to be all that God created us to be, as we follow the Lord together and fulfill our destinies as a kingdom couple. "The buck stops here" implies that this is the person who ultimately has to take responsibility for the outcome of the operations. That can be a heavy load. A leader who is comfortable with the knowledge that "the buck stops here" has confidence in his abilities and knows he has the confidence of the people under him. In the home, our husbands hold the position where the buck stops. They very much need to know that their wives see them as being up to the task. The Lord wouldn't instruct us as He does in 1 Peter 3:2, if our husbands didn't need for us to interact with them in that way. We are one with our husbands. If it is a blessing to them, it is surely a blessing for us too!

Termites can eat away at the foundation of a home for a while before the owners may become aware of the destruction that has been going on right under their noses. When you are coaching your husband by giving unsolicited advice or just plain telling him what to do, it may seem for a while that there hasn't been any damage to his confidence or to the marriage relationship. However, just as the termites can be secretly destroying your home, your coaching can be destroying something precious in your husband and your relationship with him that may not be immediately detectable. If you have been regularly coaching your husband and you think you've been getting away with it, think again! He may not feel as good about himself as he once did and he definitely doesn't feel as good about you! God tells us as wives to honor our husbands because they *need* to be honored. Your husband doesn't want to feel as if he's married to his mother. He wants to be married to his beauty to rescue. Even if you are advising him in what seems to you like a positive way, it feels to him as if the beauty thinks *he* needs rescuing. Your relationship is out of God's order. Think of it this way. How would you feel if your knight in shining armor expected you to pursue him? And to make matters worse, when you pursued him, he resisted you and ran away? Not so good? That is because your relationship would be out of order. It wouldn't fit the desire you have in your heart. If you are realizing that you've not been doing so well in your cheerleader role, keep reading and be encouraged! As you submit to God and ask for His help in becoming a 1 Peter 3 wife, He can start restoring what has been lost. God is in the business of damage control. He will show you how to honor your husband!

If shown a notebook-sized sheet of blank white paper, except for an eraser-sized black dot and asked, "What do you see?" most of us would say, "a little black dot." Although the paper is 99% white, most would focus on the dot. That erroneous focus can happen when looking at our husbands. We can overlook and take for granted their strengths and focus on the weaknesses that concern us. All people have faults and flaws; there are no exceptions. You may need to ask the Lord to enable you to see your husband through His eyes, which means you will see him through the eyes of love. This is a heart issue. The revering, respecting, honoring, esteeming, appreciating and prizing must be genuine. That admiration says to your husband, "I believe in you!" It conveys complete acceptance and an expectation for success. When we jump into the coaching role, our husbands do not feel honored or respected. It sends them the message that we don't have confidence in them to be the head of the household or to be successful in whatever we are trying to "be helpful" and advise them about.

When God looks at us, He sees the finished work; He sees what we will be when His work in us is completed. As Christians, we have the righteousness of Jesus and He sees us with His perfection. We need to see our husbands that way and ourselves as well! It is important that we are able to receive the unconditional love that God has for us first, and to love others with that love.

Love bears up under anything *and* everything that comes, is ever ready to believe the best of every person, its

hopes are fadeless under all circumstances and it endures everything [without weakening].

1 Corinthians 13:7

Ask the Lord to show you what to prize and admire about your husband. He may show you some things that you haven't noticed or thought of before. One attribute the Holy Spirit reminded me about my husband, Joe, is that he is very sensitive to my feelings. My tendency to cry at the drop of a hat over anything really good, really bad, really beautiful, or any other kind of extreme – doesn't annoy him in the least little bit. He accepts it as just another part of the woman he loves. Joe is never critical of me and I am completely safe to be who I am. One Sunday in the morning church service, the husband of a couple that had been married for 65 years was telling the congregation that husbands should tell their wives four times a day that they are loved. Joe called me from work that Monday to jokingly say that he didn't think he needed to tell me he loved me again until Wednesday because he had figured out that he was actually ahead of the quota. I had to agree that he is very good at sincerely saying, "I love you" and I was tickled at his humor. The wonderful attributes about your husband that have been there from the start of your relationship can sometimes go unnoticed. It is easy to take something that has never been an issue for granted.

Bottom line, you need to honor and respect your husband because of the position he has in your life. He is your head, according to God's Word. Just as we are to honor and respect our boss, our president and all of those that have been put in authority over us, we are to respect our husbands. It is a service to the Lord and ultimately we should obey this Word to honor Him!

But I want you to know *and* realize that Christ is the Head of every man, the head of a woman is her husband, and the Head of Christ is God.

1 Corinthians 11:3

In the verses below, we see that the behavior of Sarah and "other women of old" is being described as a model for us to follow. God's Word is eternal. It will always work; it doesn't change with time.

For it was thus that the pious women of old who hoped in God were [accustomed] to beautify themselves and were submissive to their husbands [adapting themselves to them as themselves secondary and dependent upon them].

It was thus that Sarah obeyed Abraham [following his guidance and acknowledging his headship over her by] calling him lord (master, leader, authority). And you are now her true daughters if you do right and let nothing terrify you [not giving way to hysterical fears or letting anxieties unnerve you].

1 Peter 3:5, 6

When God's order and plan is perfectly carried out in a marriage relationship, the husband is to love the wife as Jesus loves the church and gave Himself up for her. Under those conditions, that makes it very easy for the wife to submit to her husband. That combined with the wife's role as described above, brings perfect harmonious balance to the marriage relationship. One shouldn't be without the other. Each spouse has different responsibilities and purpose in the marriage. Of course we know that not all wives are loved or treated as they should be, but if we obey the Word to honor our husbands as a service unto the Lord, blessing will come from it. If your husband is unsaved, the Lord wants to reveal the unconditional love He has for your husband through you, when you allow God to align you with 1 Peter 3:2, and that can ultimately lead to his salvation. Sometimes we have to trust in the Lord with all of our hearts and walk by faith and not by sight. God is working in your husband's heart as you obey the Word.

At the end of 1 Peter 3:6, it speaks about not being afraid. Fear is catching and can paralyze us and cause us to be ineffective.

Faith is catching too. As we have confidence in the Lord to take care of us, as we obey His Word, our husbands will be more peaceful to carry out their responsibilities. Having faith in the Lord, as we support our husbands according to the Word, will help our husband's faith to stay strong.

For as he thinks in his heart, so is he.

Proverbs 23:7a

If our husbands believe they are capable, they are much more empowered to be so (as are we). As Christians our confidence should be that Jesus Christ is equipping us and we are up to every task *in Him.*

I have strength for all things in Christ Who empowers me [I am ready for anything and equal to anything through Him Who infuses inner strength into me; I am self-sufficient in Christ's sufficiency].

Philippians 4:13

For in Him we live and move and have our being; as even some of your [own] poets have said, For we are also His offspring.

Acts 17:28

God Is Not A Chauvinist!

Let there be no misunderstanding. All men are not over all women. It is just the husband that is the head of the wife. This relationship is to mirror Christ's relationship with us, His church. It is God's order for a beautifully functioning, happy and healthy marriage. But God is an equal opportunity employer. Women have the same spiritual authority as men do to speak in the name of Jesus and take authority over the works of the enemy. Women operate in every spiritual gift, as men do.

We are all able to receive the baptism of the Holy Spirit. Some women are prophets, some are called to teach and minister in the same power of the Lord as any man is able through the Holy Spirit. We are heirs of salvation and have all that that entails, as our Christian brothers do. We are *all* called to do the same works that Jesus did and even greater ones.

For in Christ you are all sons of God through faith.

For as many [of you] as were baptized into Christ [into a spiritual union and communion with Christ, the Anointed One, the Messiah] have put on (clothed yourselves with) Christ.

There is [now no distinction] neither Jew nor Greek, there is neither slave nor free, there is not male and female; for you are all one in Christ Jesus.

Now if you belong to Christ [are in Him Who is Abraham's Seed], then you are Abraham's offspring and [spiritual] heirs according to promise.

Galatians 3:26-29

A Prayer To Be A Wife Who Honors Your Husband

Father, I ask that you teach me how to truly honor and respect my husband in the way that my husband most needs. Please forgive me for the times I've failed. Enable me to see my husband through Your eyes. Show me what to appreciate and prize and how to convey it to him in the way that will bring him the most blessing. Teach me how to encourage him and cheer him on. Lord, use me to increase his confidence, so he will walk in victory, with his eyes on You, expecting You to add on Your abilities and power to his natural gifts and talents. Free him to be the person you have created him to be. Lord, multiply Your grace to me, as I need it. I can't do this on my own. Thank you for being my helper and taking my part. Thank you for bringing restoration to our marriage wherever it is needed! In Jesus' name. Amen.

79

For the Word that God speaks is alive and full of power (making it active, operative, energizing, and effective); it is sharper than any two-edged sword, penetrating to the dividing line of the breath of life (soul) and [the immortal] spirit, and of joints and marrow [of the deepest parts of our nature] exposing and sifting and analyzing and judging the very thoughts and purposes of the heart.

Hebrews 4:12

Chapter 3

Releasing God's Word Over Your Husband's Life

Like it or not, we are in a war against the principalities and powers of darkness (Ephesians 6:12). Jesus came that we have and enjoy life in abundance, but the devil comes to steal, kill and destroy whatever he can in the lives of God's children (John 10:10). But the weapons of our warfare are mighty for the overthrow and destruction of demonic strongholds (2 Corinthians 10:4). God's Word is the sword of the spirit. This chapter is a resource of declarations to decree and declare over your husband every day. Pray and confess God's Word over your husband's life and thank God that it is done! God's Word is alive, active and full of power (Hebrews 4:12). God's ears are open to His Word and He does what His Word says (Jeremiah 1:12). You may be calling things that be not as though they were. Wonderful! His Word has the power to change your present situation. God is bigger than anything that would hinder us in our lives and He is willing and able to set us free. As you confess God's Word, fill in your husband's name (and your own). Make it personal! God's order, will and power will be loosed over your husband's life as you speak these words of faith.

Joe and I each have the same declarations printed out in large letters at the tops of our respective bathroom mirrors with our names inserted in the appropriate places. We felt as if we were in a scary pit when Joe experienced a deep depression which I'll talk about more in the next chapter. Reading and speaking these words posted on my mirror daily enabled me to put the full weight of my cares on the Lord. These truths lifted me out of the pit to sit with Him in heavenly places (Ephesians 2:6). We are meant to sit at His table and partake of His goodness *in the presence* of our enemies (Psalm 23:5). It is in the midst of difficult times that we especially need to be able to receive His peace.

I know the plans I have for you, Mary, says the Lord; **plans for your good,** not to harm you or bring evil.
All things work for the good for Mary who loves the Lord.
God is not a man that He should lie. [God always speaks the truth.]
I AM your **Faithful and True.**
Trust in Me with all your heart and lean not to your own understanding. In all your ways acknowledge Me and I will direct your path.

Declarations Of Faith For Your Husband

When Psalm 1:1-3 and Ephesians 1:17-19 are activated in your husband's life, he will become aligned with the Lord and fulfill His plans and purposes. A Psalm 1 man is rooted in the Word of God and walks in wisdom, and prospers and endures because of it. God's Word will cause Godly priorities to be established in his life. When Ephesians 1:17-

19 is activated in your husband, he will have a revelation of Jesus, and understand who he is in Him. These two powerful scriptures along with the others below, have been adapted and paraphrased into declarations for your use! The faith declarations for you to speak over your husband have been arranged in these categories:

- His Relationship With The Lord
- His Character
- His Heart And His Words
- His Role In Our Family

In Job 22:28 God says that what you decide and decree, He will establish.

His Relationship With The Lord

Blessed is _____ who walks and lives not in the counsel of the ungodly, nor stands in the path where sinners walk, nor sits down to relax and rest where the scornful and the mockers gather.

But _____'s delight and desire are in the law of the Lord, and on the teachings of God, which he ponders and studies by day and by night.

And _____ shall be like a tree firmly planted and tended by the streams of water, ready to bring its fruit in its season; its leaf also shall not fade or wither and everything _____ does shall prosper and come to maturity.

Psalm 1:1-3

Thank you Father for granting _____ a spirit of wisdom and revelation of insight in the deep and intimate knowledge of You,

By having the eyes of _____'s heart flooded with light, so that _____ can know and understand the hope

to which He has been called, and how rich is Your glorious inheritance in the saints

And that _____ knows what is the immeasurable and surpassing greatness of Your power in and for him who believes, as demonstrated in the working of Your mighty strength.

Ephesians 1:17-19

_____ is strong in the Lord. _____ is empowered through his union with Him and draws His strength from Him.

Ephesians 6:10

_____ seeks first the kingdom of God and His righteousness and all other things needed are added to him.

Matthew 6:33

_____ trusts in You, Lord with all of his heart and leans not to his own understanding.

_____ acknowledges You in all his ways and You direct and makes straight and plain _____'s paths.

Proverbs 3: 5, 6

_____ who trusts in the Lord is compassed about with mercy and with loving kindness.

Psalm 32:10

_____ walks by faith in God and not by sight or appearance.

2 Corinthians 5:7

Lord, You will guard and keep _____ in perfect peace because his mind is stayed on You, because He commits

himself to you, leans on you, and hopes confidently in
you.

Isaiah 26:3

The Lord will instruct _____ and teach _____ in
the way that he should go; the Lord will counsel _____
with His eye upon him.

Psalm 32:8

His Character

_____ bears the fruit of the spirit which is love, joy
peace, patience, kindness, goodness, faithfulness, gentleness
and self-control.

Galatians 5:22, 23

_____ lets go of all bitterness, bad temper, resentment,
quarrelling, contention, slander, spite and ill will.
_____ is useful, helpful and kind, compassionate,
loving-hearted and forgiving to others.

Ephesians 4:31, 32

_____ walks and lives in the Holy Spirit, controlled
and guided by Him and does not gratify the desires of his
flesh.

Galatians 5:16

_____ is not selfish, conceited or arrogant, but esteems
others more highly than himself.
_____ is concerned not just for his interests, but for
the interests of others.

Philippians 2:3, 4

_____ walks in love; he is not self-seeking, touchy, fretful or resentful; he pays no attention to a suffered wrong.

_____ does not rejoice at injustice, but rejoices when truth prevails.

_____ walks in love that bears up under anything and everything that comes and endures without weakening.

1 Corinthians 13:5-7

His Heart and His Words

These declarations are so important because out of the abundance of the heart the mouth speaks (Matthew 12:34), and your husband will eat the fruit of his words (Proverbs 18:21). Those scriptures are saying that he will end up speaking what he believes in his heart. And he will bring goodness or evil into his life by the words that he speaks. So it is crucial that he is believing what God has to say in His Word and speaking God's good report! As you confess God's Word over your husband, and God performs it, God will bring your husband through a process that will transform him into a man of faith.

_____ **has the mind of Christ and the thoughts and purposes of His heart.**

1 Corinthians 2:16

_____ **keeps and guards his heart with all vigilance for out of it flows the springs of life.**

Proverbs 4:23

_____ **chooses life with his words and eats the fruit of it.**

Proverbs 18:21

_____ holds fast and retains without wavering his confession of faith.

Hebrews 10:23

_____ lets no polluting language or evil word or worthless talk come from his mouth.

Ephesians 4:29

_____ keeps himself from trouble because he guards the words that come from his mouth.

Proverbs 21:2

His Protection

Father, thank you that you contend with those that contend with _____.

Psalm 35:1

Father, you are a hiding place for _____, You, Lord, preserve _____ from trouble, You surround him with songs and shouts of deliverance.

Psalm 32:7

Thank you Lord that no evil shall befall _____ and no calamity will come near him
For You give your angels charge over him to defend and preserve him in all his ways.

Psalm 91:10, 11

No weapon formed against _____ shall prosper, and every tongue that shall rise against _____ in judgment will be shown to be in the wrong

Isaiah 54:17

Because _____ listens to the Lord, wisdom dwells securely in him and he has no fear or dread of evil.

Proverbs 1:33

Because _____ has a reverent and worshipful fear of the Lord, he rests satisfied and cannot be visited with evil.

Proverbs 19:23

His Role In Our Family

Thank you Lord, that _____ loves his wife as Jesus loves the church and gave Himself up for her.

Ephesians 5:25

Thank you Lord, that _____ is affectionate and sympathetic towards me and is not harsh, bitter or resentful.

Colossians 3:19

_____ lives considerately with me (his wife), honors me as being physically weaker and realizes that we are joint heirs of God's grace so his prayers are not hindered or cut off.

1 Peter 3:7

_____ trains up his children in the way they should go, so even when they are old they will not depart from those ways.

Proverbs 22:6

_____ does not provoke, irritate or harass his children so they do not become discouraged, frustrated or feel inferior. He does not break their spirit.

Colossians 3:21

Be strong and let your heart take courage, all you who wait for and hope for and expect the Lord!

Psalm 31:24

Chapter 4

Releasing Your Husband To The Lord

God wants you to walk in the freedom and peace that comes when you have completely released your husband to Him to do His perfect work. That is *not* something we are able to do apart from Him. On our own, in dependence on our abilities, our flesh will insist that we take situations into *our* hands, and coach our husbands as we see fit. The fear and pressure that will try to come when you are in a trial and your husband doesn't look like he's making the right choices, will cause you to make the wrong choices yourself, if your eyes are not on the Lord and the truth of 1 Peter 3 is not established in your heart. Revelation of this truth will enable you to successfully operate in your role as cheerleader for your husband. A Proverbs 31 woman only does her husband good. Without God's revelation of 1 Peter 3, your version of "good" will be skewed.

It is crucial for you to be strongly connected to the Lord and maintain a close relationship with Him because at times, you will need to be able to ignore what is going on around you – what you see and hear in the natural, and stand in faith that God's Word will prevail regardless of how the situation looks. This is really a trust issue with the Lord. Trust Him to be the kind of coach that your husband needs and you can completely turn the coaching job over to Him!

At a time when my husband, Joe, and I were in a low valley, God instructed me past many landmines of the enemy with His life-giving instruction in 1 Peter 3. To Joe, it seemed that out of no-where depression slithered in, wrapping her deathly tentacles around his mind and pulling him down into a very dark place. His job was good, our marriage was good, but hopelessness and despair flooded his soul and he was fighting for his life! Disabled by this hellish attack, he resigned from a job that he loved. We felt overwhelmed by the circumstances and fearful about what would ensue. Joe needed me to keep my advice to myself and support him in prayer through the months ahead. Without the Lord's counsel through His Word, in well-meaning attempts to help, I would have repeatedly tried to coach Joe, damaging our relationship and bringing him further down. I had to learn to release my husband to the Lord.

God showed Himself to be mighty and faithful through this time. Joe not only recovered to once again experience the joy of his salvation, but God gave him a better job than he originally had. At the end of his trial, Joe experienced the blessing of favor that deepened his faith. God slipped him into his new job just two weeks after his resume was on file on the Internet. Several steps of the usual hiring process were eliminated for him because of God's divine favor and after a twenty-five minute phone interview, Joe got the job! God sent him back to work on my birthday – a gift not lost on me! Joe had gotten his job without ever having to leave the house at a time when jobs were scarce, the economy was doing poorly, and unemployment was at an all-time high. None of these factors hindered God in bringing restoration. With Him all things are possible!

God Will Take Your Husband Through
Just The Right Process

God knows your husband intimately and loves him deeply and unconditionally. He has already planned to take your husband through just the right process to set him free to be the man he was created to be. Isaiah 28:23-29 is an allegory to help us understand that the Lord knows exactly how to shape and mold us for His desired outcome. It is talking about the wisdom from the Lord that the farmer uses in preparing his seed to be just right for sowing. The preparation and handling of the seed varies greatly according to the kind of seed. After the seed is prepared, the farmer sows the seed in its intended area in the field. The process the Lord will take us through to become the people He created us to be will also vary greatly from person to person. He needs to accomplish different things in each of us and we are quite different from each other to begin with. So the way in which God works in your life will not be the same way He needs to work in your husband's life. Only the Lord knows how to change his heart. Only the Lord knows how to speak to him to bring true revelation to what he needs to understand. A woman leading my church Bible study once said that the Lord spoke to her heart that she sees the world through pink tinted glasses and her husband sees the world through blue tinted glasses. That was God's way of letting her know that He would be able to impart wisdom into her husband to give him the needed direction in a way that she could not. Just as the farmer sows the seed into the land, when God's preparation in us is completed, He sows us into other people's lives. The Lord will have some purposes for your husband that won't be the same as yours. The process He needs to take your husband through will not be the same process He will be taking you through. But know this, if the Lord has put you two together, He is taking you both through just the right life experiences simultaneously. What the Lord wants to do in your life through a trial will be different from what He wants to accomplish in your husband's through the same trial. We know that all things are working for good for those who love God (Romans 8:28). God will turn attacks from the enemy around to use for our good. God will use *everything* for our good and His glory as we trust Him to do so. Not only do our husbands not feel respected when we try to coach, but we don't really have any idea how the coaching needs to be done to be effective for them.

When I was teaching my first graders, if I were changing a bulletin board on a day they were in the classroom for recess because of inclement weather, they would want to help me. They didn't have the manual dexterity or coordination to be of any real help. I would sometimes find a job they could do so they felt like they were helping but the truth was I was really helping them to feel useful and they were slowing me down. That's a good picture of what can happen when we are trying to help God coach our husbands. We don't have the skills to do it and we can slow down the process that we think we are helping to speed up.

A Prayer For My Husband; Releasing Him Into God's Hands

We, as wives, should be our husbands' greatest intercessors. Bring your husband before the Lord through prayer and release Him into God's hands. Acknowledge to the Lord your inability to coach. Ask Him to equip you to be a 1 Peter 3 wife so you are encouraging your husband to be all that God created him to be. It is when you have released your husband into God's hands and relinquished all control the Lord is free to move in his life. Only God can set him free to prosper in whatever area he has been struggling. Give the Lord your worries, your cares, your frustrations, your anger and your fears! Be free, woman of God! Whatever you have placed in your Father's hands is no longer your burden to bear. Once you have released it to Him, determine to keep it in His hands. Don't take it back. Keep your peace by thinking on Him, meditate on His Word and speak faith words of victory. Pray this prayer over your husband. Say his name in the blanks. Put your name in too wherever it is appropriate.

Father, I thank you that you are _____'s I Am. You are his strength, his shield, his way-maker, his wisdom, his healer, his counselor and his deliverer. Open his heart and mind to you as never before, so he is receptive and responsive to the work of your Holy Spirit. Open his ears to Your deep calling his deep. Take him out into the deepest depths he has ever known with you. Reveal Yourself to him, so he walks in the full joy of his salvation. Keep him hungry for Your presence and cause him to be a man of Your Word, so he is a Psalm 1 man who prospers at what he sets his hands to, bears fruit in due season and is as a tree whose leaves do not whither or fade. I thank you, Father, that _____ is strong in the Lord and the power of Your might; that he trusts You and leans not to his own understanding.

Father, enable _____ to lay aside every sin that would so easily beset him, so he is holy as You are holy. Thank you for endurance to run the race, vision to see the goal and hearing ears that are tuned in to Your voice. Fan the flame in his heart and cause his lamp to be full of Holy Spirit oil. Align _____ with You in his heart, mind, will and emotions. Remove all distractions, so his focus is steady and he won't be deterred from fulfilling all of Your plans and purposes. Arm _____ with unshakeable faith and boldness; that he calls things that be not as though they were. Make him a vessel that receives and pours out Your unconditional love to others.

Father, heal his heart and cause his identity to be in You. Give him a heart of thanksgiving. Help _____ to live with You in the present. Release him from regrets or pain from the past and anxiety about the future. Please remove any foolishness from his heart and give him the gift of repentance wherever he needs it. Enable him to walk in forgiveness. Give him a heart of flesh and remove any stoniness.

Father, fill _____ with a reverential fear of You, that is the beginning of all wisdom. Thank You that he honors You in word and deed. Cause _____ to be spiritually discerning so he is not deceived. Increase his confidence in You, and in the gifts that you have given him. Cause his gifts to be stirred up and fine-tuned. Cleanse him of any pride, so he comes to You with a humble and contrite heart. Cause him to operate in Your integrity.

Father, bless him as a husband and a father. Anoint and equip him to be the high priest of our home. Lead him by Your Holy Spirit and teach him how to abide in You.

Bless him on his job. Pour Your creative ideas into his mind and give him effective strategies. Give him work that is fulfilling and equip him to excel. Thank you that _____ walks in Your divine favor and he commits everything he does to You, totally relying on you as his source for all things. Thank you that _____ acknowledges all that You do for him and gives You all the glory that is Yours! Thank you that _____ has the mind of Christ and the thoughts and purposes of Your heart for every situation.

In the name of Jesus, I bind spiritual blindness, deafness and luke-warmness off of _____ and I loose blood-covered zeal, focus and fire of the Lord. I bind defeat off of _____ and I loose blood-covered success in the name of Jesus. I bind away spirits of fear or intimidation and I loose blood-covered faith and peace in the name of Jesus. I take authority over every principality and power of darkness that would hinder _____ in Jesus' name. I call every plan of the enemy null and void in his life. Jesus is Lord over _____, over his mind, heart, body and circumstances. I bind any confusion in the name of Jesus and I loose blood-covered truth and wisdom. I call forth every plan and purpose for _____'s life so when he stands before Your throne he will hear the words, "Well done good and faithful servant!"

Father, thank you that Your priorities are established in _____'s life. Thank you for filling his heart with Your desires. Father, revive him, and restore anything that has ever been stolen from his life.

Father, thank you for being _____'s coach. Thank you that You counsel and instruct him in the way he should go. I release _____ into your hands that You do Your perfect work in him. I trust You! I believe You! I thank You! I praise You! I love You! All this I pray in the name of Jesus. Amen.

Salvation Prayer For An Unsaved Husband

Father, I bring _____ before You. Lord, open up his eyes to his need for a savior. Give him the gift of repentance so he is able to come to You with a humble and contrite heart. Lord, make him hungry for You. Reveal Yourself to him so he knows who You are and how much You love him. Thank you for preparing his heart and drawing him to You. Thank you for sending the right people to speak into his life. I declare that in agreement with Your Word, I and my household are saved. In the name of Jesus, I bind Satan and loose _____ to the convicting call of the Holy Spirit. Thank you that _____ is receptive and responsive to Your perfect work in his life. I speak a divine revelation of wisdom and understanding of Jesus Christ over _____. I see my husband as saved and serving You with all of his heart. Help me to walk by faith and *not by sight*. Thank You for Your faithfulness! In Jesus' name. Amen.

Even if your husband is not yet saved and serving the Lord, pray the first prayer over him too. You will be calling forth God's full purposes for him. As you continue to pray these prayers over your husband, thank the Lord that each of these requests have been answered. God answers the first time that you pray with a definite, reliable yes! The manifestation of the answers can be a process that happens over time. Ask God to help you to see it as finished and for grace to continue to release your faith. Each time you pray, more walls of resistance are being weakened and coming down! Satan's power sometimes seems mighty but God is *almighty!* It is like comparing the flame of a match to the sun. In Christ, you will prevail.

The earnest (heartfelt, continued) prayer of a righteous man makes tremendous power available [dynamic in its working].

James 5:16b

Part 3

Activation Of God's Power In Your Life

For All Women

Introduction

Activation Of God's Power In Your Life

We don't begin an exercise program by hiking up Mt. Everest. The climber who makes it to the mountain top has spent much time in preparation. He is equipped with the knowledge of how to survive in adverse conditions and is prepared for any number of what could be unforeseen life-threatening scenarios. His preparation goes way beyond knowledge. It goes beyond having the right equipment. He has already been on numerous hiking experiences that have prepared him for this ultimate test. He is a seasoned hiker who is armed with wisdom learned along the way that will shield him from what could be fatal mistakes. His body is in peak condition, his mind is ready to discern when an immediate decision for a change in course is required, his state-of-the-art equipment is carefully assembled, and he is primed for this adventure with a strong "I can!" mindset.

There will be mountains before us in our lives that look insurmountable. Those mountains may be emotional mountains of pain from past life experiences that have brought great trauma and feelings of hopelessness and disappointment. They may be physical in the form of a disease or some kind of disability. There may be mountains of dysfunction in relationships or of lack in financial situations. Mountains that seemingly block the way to having our deepest heart's desires realized sometimes loom before us. But if you are a child of the almighty God, *you were born to be the mountain climber who makes it to the top!* –Not just to the top of one mountain, but to the top of many

99

mountains! *You were born* to have feet as hinds' feet, sure-footed and steady, able to successfully navigate around the narrow rocky ledges.

He makes my feet like hinds' feet [able to stand firmly or make progress on the dangerous heights of testing and trouble]; He sets me securely upon high places.

Psalm 18:33

You may be reading this thinking, "But I'm just an ordinary person," and that is the truth. Without the Lord we are all just ordinary people. *But in Him* you are more than a conqueror. *In Him*, you are an overcomer. *You were born* to function and live in this truth: "I can do all things through Christ Who strengthens me." *You were born* to abide in and be vitally connected to The Maker Of Heaven And Earth, The Faithful And True, The Great I Am , The Almighty God Who is King Of Kings and Lords Of Lords! The knowledge we must have to make it to the top comes from revelation of the Word of God. Without that preparation in His Word, many mountains in our lives can never be conquered. Every mountain in a believer's life is conquered by faith, faith in God and His Word, and obedience to His voice. The necessary gear will fit you perfectly.

Therefore put on God's complete armor, that you may be able to resist *and* stand your ground on the evil day [of danger], and, having done all [the crisis demands], to stand [firmly in your place].

Stand therefore [hold your ground], having tightened the belt of truth around your loins and having put on the breastplate of integrity *and* of moral rectitude *and* right standing with God.

And having shod your feet in preparation [to face the enemy with the firm-footed stability, the promptness, and the readiness produced by the good news] of the Gospel of peace.

Lift up over all the [covering] shield of saving faith, upon which you can quench all the flaming missiles of the wicked [one].

And take the helmet of salvation and the sword that the Spirit wields, which is the Word of God.

Ephesians 6:13-17

It will be God's wisdom spoken to your heart by His Holy Spirit that will lead you in the way you should go. God will not just show you the way, He *is* The Way. He is your Way-Maker. Every promise in His Word is for you and *it is possible* for the fulfillment of that Word in your life.

For with God nothing is ever impossible *and* no word from God shall be without power *or* impossible of fulfillment.

Luke 1:37

Just as God clothed Gideon with Himself He will clothe you. Gideon was a fearful man but through God's supernatural power and anointing he was used to bring a great victory for Israel.

But the Spirit of the Lord clothed Gideon with Himself *and* took possession of him, and he blew a trumpet, and [the clan of] Abiezer was gathered to him.

Judges 6:34

The fact that there have been failures and set-backs in your life is absolutely no indication that you will not be the conqueror of many mountains! Do not listen to the disheartening lies of the enemy! He knows well the victorious power that becomes available in the life of a believer through the salvation experience when our Father-child relationship is established with God. He knows eventual victory is assured for you when God's Word becomes activated in your life and you are operating in spiritual oneness with Him. God has planned many adventures before you to bring opportunity in your life to use His spiritual tools, to grow up in Him, and to plant seeds of faith that will enable you to climb some mountains in your future.

Each life experience, whether one of victory or defeat, will be used for your ultimate good because you love the Lord (Romans 8:28). Only God can bring restoration and healing to circumstances that have brought great devastation to our lives. Sometimes we have to determine to say, "I don't know why that happened. God, I don't understand, but I know that you are good and your Word is true."

The third part of this book is to further equip and encourage you to believe God to be your match-maker, and/or equip you to be your husband's cheerleader trusting Him to be the Coach, *and* to better equip you to climb whatever mountains are ahead. My prayer is that my God-adventures will be faith seeds planted in your hearts for future mountain climbing experiences with Him.

Now to Him Who, by (in consequence of) the [action of His] power that is at work within us, is able to [carry out His purposes and] do superabundantly, far over *and* above all that we [dare] ask or think [infinitely beyond our highest prayers, desires, thoughts, hopes or dreams]—

To Him be glory in the church and in Christ Jesus throughout all generations forever and ever. Amen (so be it).

Ephesians 3:20

Because if you acknowledge and confess with your lips that Jesus is Lord and in your heart believe (adhere to, trust in, and rely on the truth) that God raised Him from the dead, you will be saved.

For with the heart a person believes (adheres to, trusts in, and relies on Christ) and so is justified (declared righteous, acceptable to God), and with the mouth he confesses (declares openly and speaks out freely his faith) and confirms [his] salvation.

Romans 10:9, 10

Chapter 1

Getting On God's Plan For Your Whole Life

God has a plan for your whole life that encompasses the husband-situation and so much more! The first step to getting on this plan is to make Jesus your Lord and Savior. He desires to have a personal relationship with you! The first five chapters in this book could happen only because I got on God's plan for my life. I grew up going to Sunday school and knowing that Jesus loved me. I loved Him. I remember one time as a child, feeling a sickly fear and crying out to God for help when my little brother was ill as I crouched down on the floor in our bathroom and prayed. My Sunday school teachers gave us a sticker on a red ribbon chart each Sunday after we whispered the memorized verse for the week in their ear. The one that helps me to this day is *I will trust and not be afraid Isaiah 12:2.* Although I knew that Jesus died for our sins, I was never taught that there needs to be a response on my part to receive the free gift of salvation. I made that response when some ladies involved in Campus

Crusade For Christ led me in a salvation prayer when I was a sophomore at Illinois State University in 1974.

Unknowledgeable about God's Word and not being involved in any activities that would bring spiritual growth, I was a spiritual baby for years. In the early 1980s one of my close friends introduced me to the teachings of Kenneth and Gloria Copeland and Kenneth Hagan. I devoured books written by those teachers of faith, listened to their tapes and watched the *Believer's Voice Of Victory* on television.

The foundational teachings of my Christian walk came from the exposure to these ministries. I gained understanding about aspects of God's whole salvation gift that I had known nothing about such as the power of our words, the principles of faith, sowing and reaping and divine healing. *Casting Your Cares Upon the Lord* and *the name of* JESUS by Kenneth Hagin as well as a number of his books on divine healing were life changing for me. God planted more seeds for the healing ministry when I went to Gloria Copeland's Healing School at a Kenneth Copeland Believers' Convention in Fort Worth, Texas, in the late 80s. I'll never forget witnessing a crippled boy who couldn't stand without being held up. He was instantly healed and racing around the auditorium at one of Kenneth's evening services.

Paying a tithe (giving a tenth of your gross income to the Lord) always seemed like a huge amount to give until I read Gloria's book, *God's Will Is Prosperity,* giving me the freedom to obey the Lord with my finances. God used that book to show me it is impossible to out give Him and I can't afford *not* to tithe and miss out on the blessings God has in return for my obedience. It is a wise believer who not only tithes to her church but gives seeds offerings into ministries that God is using to bring ministry into her life.

Watching the 700 Club became a part of my nightly routine and I prayed in agreement with those on the show as they operated in the spiritual gifts of the word of knowledge and word of wisdom. I finally visited a spirit-filled church in the late 80s although I had never been in a service when the gifts referred to in 1 Corinthians 12:7-11 were in operation. However, because of what I had learned from my reading and Christian television, I understood exactly what was going on and was hungry to experience God's presence in a deeper way. When I finally started attending a small spirit-filled church, I knew I was in a place where God's supernatural gifts were believed in and allowed to flow as the Holy Spirit led. Just weeks after beginning to attend that church, I brought one of my friends who was in great need of healing in her stomach and eyes. Without letting anyone in the church know of her need, I believed for God to speak to the pastor to call people to the front who needed prayer. God heard my heart's cry and answered in a powerful way. The pastor did ask people to come to the front to be healed, an action which he had never taken before when I had been present. God miraculously touched my friend in both parts of her body and healing came! God used the experience of my friend's healing to draw me into a deeper desire to see people healed and set free in every area of their lives. He was even then preparing me to be a part of the healing ministry at Guiding Light Ministries Healing Rooms in Decatur.

He had taught me to expect Him to be faithful to His Word through the books He'd had me read. Through those teachings on the Word of God He was building my faith. By the time I read the book, *God Is A Match-Maker* by Derek and Ruth Prince, I already knew God as one Who loves me unconditionally, is faithful to His Word, cares about every detail of our lives and is wanting to meet the deep desires He has put in our hearts if we will only believe. Looking back, I am able to see that God had carefully planned the preparation for my faith journey with Him as my match-maker.

The God who made the universe loves you and has specific plans for your life too! Included in those plans is making the way for you to have the assurance that you will spend eternity in heaven with Him. God has made it clear through His Word, that He is a holy God and it is not possible for us to be good enough to go to heaven.

> **...and all our righteousness (our best deeds of rightness and justice) is like filthy rags *or* a polluted garment;...**
> **Isaiah 64:6b**

But God gave His only son, Jesus, to pay the price for your sin and mine so that through faith in Him, we can receive the gift of salvation. It is not through anything that you do, but because of what Jesus did for you, which was to pay the penalty for your sin by going to the cross.

> **For God so greatly loved *and* dearly prized the world that He [even] gave up His only begotten (unique) Son, so that whoever believes in (trusts in, clings to, relies on) Him shall not perish (come to destruction, be lost) but have eternal (everlasting) life.**
> **John 3:16**

> **Since all have sinned and are falling short of the honor and glory which God bestows and receives**
> **[All] are justified and made upright *and* in right standing with God, freely and gratuitously by His grace (His unmerited favor and mercy), through the redemption which is [provided] in Christ.**
> **Whom God put forward [before the eyes of all] as a mercy seat *and* propitiation by His blood [the cleansing and life-giving sacrifice of atonement and reconciliation to be received] through faith. This was to show God's righteousness, because in His divine forbearance He had passed over *and* ignored former sins without punishment.**
> **It was to demonstrate and prove at the present time (in the now season) that He Himself is righteous and that**

He justifies *and* accepts as righteous him who has [true] faith in Jesus.

Romans 3:23-26

For the wages which sin pays is death, but the [bountiful] free gift of God is eternal life through (in union with) Jesus Christ our Lord.

Romans 6:23

For there [is only] one God, and [only] one Mediator between God and men the Man Christ Jesus.

1 Timothy 2:5

For Christ [the Messiah Himself] died for sins once for all, the Righteous for the unrighteous (the Just for the unjust, the Innocent for the guilty), that He might bring us to God. In His human body He was put to death, but He was made alive in the spirit.

1 Peter 3:18

But God shows *and* clearly proves His [own] love for us by the fact that while we were still sinners; Christ (the Messiah, the Anointed One) died for us.

Romans 5:8

I am the Door; anyone who enters in through Me will be saved (will live).

John 10:9a

For it is by free grace (God's unmerited favor) that you are saved (delivered from judgment *and* made partakers of Christ's salvation) through [your] faith. And this [salvation] is not of yourselves [of your own doing it came not through your own striving], but it is the gift of God;

Not because of works [not the fulfillment of the Law's demands], lest any man should boast. [It is not the result of

what anyone can possibly do, so no one can pride himself
in it or take glory to himself.]

Ephesians 2:8, 9

God has given us all the freedom of choice. You can choose
Jesus, or not! So receiving the free gift of salvation requires a
response on your part. You need to ask Him into your heart.

Behold, I stand at the door and knock; if anyone hears
and listens to *and* heeds My voice and opens the door I
will come in to him and will eat with him, and he [will
eat] with me.

Revelation 3:20

For everyone who calls upon the name of the Lord
[invoking Him as Lord] will be saved.

Romans 10:13

A Prayer To Receive Jesus As Your Lord And Savior

Jesus, come into my heart and be Lord of my life. Make
my life what you want it to be. Help me to walk with you.
Forgive me for my sins. Thank you for saving me! Thank you
for teaching me, protecting me and healing me! Thank you that
the angels are rejoicing that my name is written in the Lamb's
book of life. Amen.

What's Next?

It is important that you have fellowship with other believers
and get connected to a church where you will be able to grow
in your knowledge of the Lord and in your relationship with
Him. Ask God to lead you to the church where He would have
you to go.

God's Word (the Bible) is Holy Spirit inspired (Timothy 3:16). Jesus *is* the Word (John 1:1). That is why the Word of God is alive and powerful (Hebrews 4:12). It is God's love letter to you. It will teach, encourage, strengthen and correct you. Faith comes from hearing the Word of God (Romans 10:17). The more time you spend in the Word, the more its truth will become your reality. God will lead, guide and direct you successfully through many difficult situations, through instruction from His Word. God will use His Word to equip you to live in victory. God said that His people perish for lack of knowledge (Hosea 4:6). Many Christians make choices that lead to grave consequences because they don't know what God's Word says about their situation. You will more deeply come to know who God is, and who you are in Christ, through His Word. Through God's Word, you'll walk in wisdom and faith to depend completely on Jesus and turn every situation over to Him. He *will* intervene on your behalf!

Another key to developing intimacy with the Lord is to spend time in prayer. It says to begin with praise, have an attitude of gratitude. Thank Him for the blessings you have. Give Him time to speak to your heart. He will bring you to a place where you recognize His voice. Pour your heart out to Him and cast every care on Him. Put on some worship music and soak in His presence!

If you live in me [abide vitally united to Me] and My words remain in you *and* continue to live in your hearts, ask whatever you will, and it shall be done for you.
John 15:7

Jesus came that you have life abundantly (John 10:10). Please continue reading Part 3, Chapter 2 to learn about being equipped to live a victorious life. It is through God's grace that you change into the person He created you to be. He doesn't expect you to change in any way through your own abilities.

As you surrender your life to Him, He will keep making adjustments that set you free in every area of your life.

And I am convinced *and* sure of this very thing, that He Who began a good work in you will continue until the day of Jesus Christ [right up to the time of His return], developing [that good work] *and* perfecting *and* bringing it to full completion in you.

Philippians 1:6

Yet amid all these things we are more than conquerors and gain a surpassing victory through Him Who loved us.

Romans 8:37

Chapter 2

Gaining A Surpassing Victory

God wants to equip you with spiritual tools so you can attain the surpassing victory He has for you (Romans 8:37)! It isn't enough just to know what God has to say about something. The knowledge of His Word needs to be *activated by faith!* This is not just about positive thinking. Faith is a spiritual force that God created. He is the author and finisher of your faith (Hebrews 12:2). God wants to align you with Him in your heart by renewing your mind with His thoughts through the washing of the Word of God (Ephesians 5:26). For years I never read the Bible because I knew the Christmas and Easter stories and thought that was all I needed to know. Perhaps because of my grandmother's prayers, I eventually felt the pull to come in deeper with Him. As I followed His lead in my heart to seek Him, He brought me into the understanding that the Bible isn't just a collection of good stories. It is *the* manual for life. Jesus is the Word of God (John 1:1). *He* will position you to move forward into victory as you form that vital connection to Him. He is your way-maker. As you read this chapter, invite the Holy Spirit to teach you and impart revelation of His Word.

Adverse circumstances will come. What you believe, do and say in response to them is a key factor that determines the final outcome. God says in His Word that *you* are to stir yourself up in the most holy faith (Jude 1:20) because God is moved by faith. *You* are responsible for protecting your mind and heart from negative thoughts that will take you out of agreement with what God has to say in His Word. Negative thoughts come but you need to replace them with the right ones. Take control of your thought life and determine to replace every negative thought with a positive confession of faith! If you don't, you can be defeated by your own words and actions that are agreeing with the enemy's negative report. As God's child, you should not be bound in your beliefs to what would normally happen without God's intervention. *God expects you to expect Him to intervene!* We often live below His provision because we have limited Him through lack of knowledge of His Word or because of not believing it. God says that His people perish because of lack of knowledge (Hosea 4:6). Failure to experience eventual victory in a situation can be due to a lack of knowledge and understanding of how God would have you respond to those adverse circumstances. God doesn't change. He is ready, willing and able to bring you to a place of surpassing victory. Are you knowledgeable about how to respond in a way that allows Him to move in power on your behalf?

Making Jesus your Lord and Savior is prerequisite to walking in all that the Lord has for you. If you have not yet done that, see chapter 1 in part 3: "Getting On God's Whole Plan For Your Life." If Jesus is yours and you are His, it is time to come out into the deep. He has more for you!

God wants you to abide in Him! Abiding denotes close relationship! Connection to the Lord through close relationship is an absolute must for victory over Satan's attacks. The more we completely depend on Him, the more He will be able to work in our lives.

Dwell in Me, and I will dwell in you, [Live in Me, and I will live in you.] Just as no branch can bear fruit of

itself without abiding in (being vitally united to) the vine, neither can you bear fruit unless you abide in me.

John 15:4

We are powerless to overcome many of the circumstances that we come up against in life. We cannot deliver ourselves. We need a deliverer! God is never caught off guard, thrown off course, or lacking the know-how, resources, or ability to turn what appears to be a sure defeat into an all-out victory.

For with God nothing is ever impossible *and* no word from God shall be without power *or* impossible of fulfillment.

Luke 1:37

If abiding in God is the key to living the abundant live that Jesus has promised us, then the knowledge of how to do that is surely of great value! How does this abiding happen? What do we do to connect with the maker of the universe Who desires to be the lover of our souls? And what knowledge has He given us through instruction in His Word? The Biblical answers to these questions are addressed in this chapter and have been organized under these headings:

- Spend Time In His Presence
- Put It All In His Hands
- Come Into Agreement With God's Word
- Know How To Respond To The Enemy's Threats
- Exercise Your Spiritual Authority
- Have A Right Heart
- Connect to Other Believers

Spend Time In His Presence

God says that you are able to have the mind of Christ and thoughts and purposes of His heart through Holy Spirit

113

revelation (2 Corinthians 2:12-16). Having a right heart and accurate thinking positions you for victory. That revelation cannot come without spending time in the presence of the Lord. Apart from Him you can do nothing. So just how do you come into His presence?

Praise and Worship

Enter into His gates with thanksgiving *and* a thank offering and into His courts with praise! Be thankful and say so to Him, bless *and* affectionately praise His name!
Psalm 100:4a

Begin by thanking Him for your salvation and the blessings in your life. Worship Him for who He is to you according to His Word. Put on a worship CD and worship Him with all your heart. Your problems will shrink as He is magnified!

I love You fervently *and* devotedly, O Lord my Strength.
The Lord is my Rock, my Fortress, and my Deliverer; my God, my keen and firm Strength in Whom I will trust and take refuge, my Shield, and the Horn of my salvation, my High Tower.
I will call upon the Lord, Who is to be praised; so shall I be saved from my enemies.
Psalm 18:1-3

Praise and worship will bring you into God's presence and is a powerful weapon against the enemy, as you saw from my story in chapter one of part one about the light of the Lord engulfing my bedroom. God inhabits the praises of His people (Psalm 22:3). Praise Him in the midst of your trial! You cannot stay in faith without keeping an attitude of gratitude. Stay thankful for who He is and for His provision. Being thankful will help you to stay in God's presence. Paul and

Silas had plenty to be fearful and disillusioned about when they were in prison, but rather than focusing on their problem they focused on the Lord. The praise and worship that flowed from their hearts brought God's power on the scene (Acts 16). The account below, from Chronicles, is another example of the power of God being ushered in through the praises of His people.

You shall not need to fight in this battle; take your positions and stand still, and see the deliverance of the Lord [Who is] with you, O Judah and Jerusalem. Fear not nor be dismayed. Tomorrow go out against them for the Lord is with you.

And Jehoshaphat bowed his head and his face to the ground, and all Judah and the inhabitants of Jerusalem fell down before the Lord worshiping Him.

And some Levites of the Kohathites and Korahites stood up to praise the Lord, the God of Israel, with a very loud voice.

And they rose early in the morning and went out into the Wilderness of Tekoa; and as they went out, Jehoshaphat stood and said, Hear me, O Judah, and you inhabitants of Jerusalem! Believe in the Lord your God *and* you shall be established; believe and remain steadfast to His prophets and you shall prosper.

When he had consulted with the people, he appointed singers to sing to the Lord and praise Him in their holy [priestly] garments as they went out before the army saying, Give thanks to the Lord, for His mercy *and* loving-kindness endures forever!

And when they began to sing and to praise, the Lord set ambushments against the men of Ammon, Moab, and Mount Seir who had come against Judah, and they were [self-] slaughtered;

For [suspecting betrayal] the men of Ammon and Moab rose against those of Mount Seir, utterly destroying

them. And when they had made an end of the men of Seir, they all helped to destroy one another.

And when Judah came to the watchtower of the wilderness, they looked at the multitude, and behold, they were dead bodies fallen to the earth and none had escaped!

When Jehoshaphat and his people came to take the spoil, they found among them much cattle, goods, garments, and precious things which they took for themselves, more than they could carry away, so much they were three days in gathering the spoil.

On the fourth day they assembled in the Valley of Beracah. There they blessed the Lord. So the name of the place is still called the Valley of Beracah [blessing].

Then they returned, every man of Judah and Jerusalem, Jehoshaphat leading them, to Jerusalem with joy, for the Lord had made them to rejoice over their enemies.

2 Chronicles 20:17-27

The praise brought the power of God that brought defeat to their enemies. The praise came first, and then their enemies were conquered! Praise and thank the Lord for His provision when you ask Him for it. Then believe that you have received it from Him by faith. Notice that after the defeat of their enemies, restoration began. God will restore what the enemy has stolen from you (Joel 2:25). In this account about Jehoshaphat, they were overwhelmed with blessings that were too many for them even to carry away, and it took three days just to gather all the spoil. Praise and thank the Lord until you see the answer and then praise and thank Him some more!

Prayer

Ask the Holy Spirit to take over your prayer time. He *will* teach you, counsel you and give you direction in the way that will most speak to your heart. Expect to hear from the Lord. Be patient and wait for Him. God already knows about all of your concerns, but He is waiting for you to turn them over to Him in prayer. Then start thanking Him for the answers. You may not know the answers or see any indication that they are coming, but receive the answers by faith when you pray. Ask the Lord to increase your faith to walk in His grace and abide in Him. Rehearsing the problem as you pray is not effective prayer because it isn't a prayer of faith. Faith sees the finished work. When Jesus was on the cross, He spoke the words "It is finished," meaning the price necessary to purchase salvation for all and all that that entails had been paid because He had willingly given His life for us. Now the provision that you need is already yours and it is being brought into the earth to be manifested in your circumstances to meet that need through your prayer of faith. In the Lord's Prayer, it says "thy kingdom come, thy will be done on earth as it is in heaven." You are calling your needed provision down to earth in the Lord's Prayer. Be specific: Come thy kingdom! Be done thy will in my husband's life, for example. Now know that the answer is on its way.

If you ordered a new sofa from a reputable furniture store, and they had guaranteed you that they would deliver it to your home, would you call them every few days to ask them to please deliver the sofa to your home? Of course you wouldn't! But many of us do that to the Lord all the time in our prayers. He remembers the first time that you asked. Thank Him for it and if the Holy Spirit brings other things to mind to pray for the situation, do so, but you don't need to start all over as though you hadn't already discussed it with Him. Isn't your Lord much more reliable than the furniture store? You *can* trust Him with your life and you can trust Him to work in the lives of the people that you are praying for.

Pray in God's Word as the Lord brings you scriptures. You will be praying in His perfect will and releasing the power of His word over your situation or people you are praying for. As you spend more time in His Word, you will begin to notice scriptures that apply to your needs. Highlight them and begin speaking them in prayer. You will be speaking and seeing your needed answers by faith as you pray the Word.

God has instructed us to pray in the name of Jesus. It is as though Jesus, Himself, is making the request to our Heavenly Father when you pray in His name. You are invited to come boldly to His throne of grace for help in your time of need (Hebrews 4:16).

Up to this time you have not asked a [single] thing in My Name [as presenting all that I Am]; but now ask *and* keep on asking and you will receive, so that your joy (gladness, delight) may be full *and* complete.

At that time you will ask (pray) in My Name; and I am not saying that I will ask the Father on your behalf [for it will be unnecessary].

John 16:24, 26

Prayer is a vital component of being connected to the Lord. God wants to intervene on your behalf in answer to your prayers.

In conclusion, be strong in the Lord [be empowered through your union with Him]; draw your strength from Him [that strength which His boundless might provides].

Pray at all times (on every occasion, in every season) in the Spirit, with all [manner of] prayer and entreaty. To that end keep alert and watch with strong purpose *and* perseverance, interceding in behalf of all the saints (God's consecrated people).

Ephesians 6:10, 18

Put It All In His Hands

When I was just beginning my teaching career, I was on my way home for a weekend visit. Just as I was nearing the exit, I thought that I was hearing a close helicopter overhead and I began looking up. Within a few seconds, the uneven rolling of my tires lead me to realize that there was no helicopter, but it was my flat tire making the almost deafening noise. I continued to drive, hoping to make it to a nearby Dairy Queen. Rolling in on the rim, I got out of the car, went into the Dairy Queen and called my dad. At that point my problem was gone because I had turned it over to my dad. The instant the communication had been completed, I knew that everything was as good as taken care of. Was the problem still there? Of course it was, but now it was no longer my problem. Now, my dad was the one with the problem. That is how it is when we are abiding in Jesus. Because of that close connection, we are able to trust Him completely and we are able to turn a problem over to Him and walk away in peace. Although the problem is still there, it is no longer ours.

We need to be able to cast every care upon Him and confidently say, "God, now You have a problem! And thank you for taking care of it for me!" 1 Peter 3 talks about our need to have the charm of a gentle and peaceful spirit.

> **Let not yours be the [merely] external adorning with [elaborate] interweaving and knotting of the hair, the wearing of jewelry, or changes of clothes;**
>
> **But let it be the inward adorning *and* beauty of the hidden person of the heart, with the incorruptible *and* unfading charm of a gentle and peaceful spirit, which [is not anxious or wrought up, but] is very precious in the sight of God.**
>
> **1 Peter: 3:4**

A woman who has a gentle and peaceful spirit is a woman whose eyes are on the Lord and whose trust is in Him. Our peace can remain in the midst of adverse circumstances when Jesus is our source. Pray about everything and know that He will answer you and intervene in your circumstances.

You will guard him *and* keep him in perfect *and* constant peace whose mind [both its inclination and its character] is stayed on You, leans on You, *and* hopes confidently in You.

So trust in the Lord (commit yourself to Him, lean on Him, hope confidently in Him) forever; for the Lord God is an everlasting Rock [the Rock of Ages].

Isaiah 26:3, 4

Come Into Agreement With God's Word

It isn't possible to have the intimate relationship with the Lord and know Him as we need to, without spending time in His Word. His Word is our standard for truth and reveals Who He is. He gives clear direction on how to handle life's situations in His Word. Counsel and instruction will come to you through His Word. God's will is in His word and His comfort and strength flows through it. When we abide in the Lord with knowledge of His Word, He is able to position us in our hearts and minds for victory.

The reason a Psalm 1 man has "leaves that don't wither or fade, bears fruit in due season and prospers at what he sets his hands to" is because he is meditating on God's Word. His focus on God's Word causes faith to come. God responds to his faith and prospers him. He has a part in his victory and God has a part. It is not his responsibility to prosper himself! As he renews his mind with the washing of the Word, replacing the enemy's negative report with the truth of God's power to overcome, he is coming into agreement with the Lord. God's part is to intervene and bring the prosperity.

Having my mind renewed with the Word of God in the midst of difficult circumstances has been the difference between despair and peace. Sometimes our *only* hope is in Him. My God of all comfort (2 Corinthians 1:3) has often led me to take refuge in the Psalms and be reminded of His power to deliver. Psalms 1, 18, 27, 32, 91 and 118 are favorites that have rescued me from fear and brought a return of sweet peace again and again.

If you live in Me [abide vitally united to Me] and My words remain in you *and* continue to live in your hearts, ask whatever you will, and it shall be done for you.
John 15:7

What you think on affects what you believe and what you speak. Thinking on what God has to say in His Word brings accurate thinking. Your thoughts will line up with Him. It brings faith that wipes out the pictures the enemy is trying to paint in your mind. If you focus on negative thoughts, your words will mirror them. You can tear down your marriage with your words. "My husband is lazy. He never does anything around our house!" It is important to align your thinking with God's promises and *speak words of life.* "Thank you God that my husband sees what needs to be done at home and he has a desire to do it! " Faith comes from hearing God's Word (Romans 10:17). As you spend time in the Word, faith will grow in your heart. It will become your truth and you will begin seeing situations through God's eyes and speaking the right words.

For the rest, brethren, whatever is true, whatever is worthy of reverence *and* is honorable *and* seemly, whatever is just, whatever is pure, whatever is lovely *and* lovable whatever is kind *and* winsome *and* gracious, if there is any virtue *and* excellence, if there is anything worthy of praise, think on and weigh and take account of these things [fix your minds on them].
Philippians 4:8

From the above scripture it is clear that we need to be positive and think on what is a good report. When we think on

God's Word as it applies to our situation, faith will grow in our hearts. Matthew 12:34 reminds us that what we believe in our hearts is what will be coming out of our mouths. Our words are little containers of power. We need to speak words of life over our husbands and the situations we are in.

Death and life are in the power of the tongue, and they who indulge in it shall eat the fruit of it [for death or life].

Proverbs 18:21

God created the earth by speaking it into existence. When He said, "Let there be light," there was light (Genesis 1:3). We are made in His image and we bring things into existence through the words of our mouth - good and bad! God calls things that be not as though they were (Romans 4:17). We should be doing the same. When we declare God's Word over our situation, we are calling things that be not as though they were. One Sunday evening at a healing service at our church, a woman named Brenda gave her testimony of how God had dramatically healed her of rheumatoid arthritis after suffering with it for three years. She went from being confined to a wheelchair to riding a bike in one afternoon. The important point that she drew us to focus on in her story was that she refused ever to say that she had arthritis. She refused to let her words line up with the enemy's plan. God's Word says that by the stripes of Jesus we are healed (Isaiah 53:5). She declared for three years that by the stripes of Jesus she was healed. She would not take possession of a disease that Jesus had already paid the price of her healing for, with the words of her mouth. She knew that the illness was trespassing and had no right to be in her body. It was a fact that rheumatoid arthritis was in her body and she did not deny that the doctors had diagnosed her with that disease. But the truth was that Jesus had already healed her according to His Word. She chose to believe and speak His Word, the Truth. She called things that be not as though they were, and eventually the Truth changed the facts.

Here's one more example of the act of calling things that be not as though they were changing a situation from one of hopelessness to one of recovery. I was a member of a church that had lost our pastor due to a fall into sin. What had been a prosperous and growing congregation turned into a tiny group of shattered believers. We had recently built and moved into a very large building which was made to house a school and a daycare, as well as a large church. We were drowning in debt with no foreseeable way out. The Lord sent us a pastor who refused ever to come into agreement with the enemy with his words concerning the building or our dismal financial state. I heard him say with complete assurance, week after week, "This building is sold in Jesus' name!" The special education district decided to purchase the property later that year and used it to house their offices as well as a school for special needs children. I'm sure one of the reasons the Lord was able to deliver us from what looked like an insurmountable problem was that our pastor held fast to his confession of faith. He didn't walk by sight, but spoke a good report in the name of Jesus. We need to speak a good report in the name of Jesus over our husbands, our marriages and all situations.

According to Matthew 12:34, what is in your heart is what will be coming out of your mouth. Filling your hearts with the Word of God will cause you to speak words of life. Whatever you really believe is what you end up saying. Your mind needs to be renewed to God's Word, so God can align your thinking with Him. As you can see in Job 22:28 below, what you speak will be established. Are you speaking words of life?

If you lay gold in the dust, and the gold of Ophir among the stones of the brook [considering them of little worth], And make the Almighty your gold and [the Lord] your precious silver treasure,

Then you will have delight in the Almighty and you
will lift up your face to God,
You will make your prayers to Him, and He will hear
you and you will pay your vows,
You shall also decide *and* decree a thing, and it shall
be established for you; and the light [of God's favor] shall
shine upon your ways.

Job 22:24-28

God's Word reminds us not to murmur or complain. If you
are complaining and reciting the negatives about your husband's
actions or your marriage relationship, you are coming into
agreement with Satan's plan and speaking word curses that will
block God's blessing. You don't want to eat the fruit of those
words! Your own frustrations and fears about the situation will
increase because of your negative confession and things will
continue to take on a hopeless feel. Speak God's Word over
your husband and all of life's situations. The Truth will change
the facts as you meditate on God's Word and speak it. God
performs His Word. Speaking God's Word will also increase
your faith, and because you are now focusing on the Lord, your
peace will be restored.

If you have been speaking negative words, those are word
curses. Repent and revoke those words in the name of Jesus. Then
declare words of blessing in the name of Jesus in their place.

Know How To Respond To The Enemy's Threats

The country that wins a war has a good understanding of its
enemy and how it operates in order to conquer it. As Christians,
we know that our enemies are supernatural, as described in
Ephesians 6:12. Our enemy is Satan and all of the powers of
darkness. These are some important things that God would
have you to know about your enemy. He is a liar and a deceiver
(John 8:44). He operates through fear and tries to appear all

powerful (as the Lord *really* is), but Jesus has already disarmed him at the cross.

> **Be well balanced (temperate, sober of mind), be vigilant *and* cautious at all times; for that enemy of yours, the devil, roams around like a lion roaring [in fierce hunger], seeking someone to seize upon and devour.**
>
> **1 Peter 5:8**

Jesus is the Lion of Judah, but through deception, the devil appears as a roaring lion. Our enemy is powerful, but the Lord is *all* powerful!

> **[God] disarmed the principalities and powers that were ranged against us and made a bold display *and* public example of them, in triumphing over them in Him *and* in it [the cross].**
>
> **Colossians 2:15**

> **The thief comes only in order to steal and kill and destroy. I came that they may have *and* enjoy life, and have it in abundance (to the full, till it overflows).**
>
> **John 10:10**

The Lord has given me wisdom about how to respond to fear from the enemy again and again through the scriptures about David and Goliath. The enemy's strategy is always the same. He paints a picture of doom and gloom about your defeat by putting thoughts in your mind about exactly what he plans to do to you just as Goliath spoke to David about what he planned to do to him. He brings fear to stop you in your tracks on your faith walk. He wants you to give up, drop your spiritual weapons and run! He'll go for the jugular vein in your marriage and all things sacred to you. Whatever your Goliaths are in your marriage or any other life situations, respond as David did, with your eyes on the Lord and words of faith coming out of your mouth.

I found once when I was lying awake in the middle of the night worrying during Joe's bout with depression, that although I had spoken to fear in the name of Jesus and told it it had to go, I really couldn't get free of it until I replaced the negative thoughts with words of faith. As I quietly whispered a thank you to God that He was taking care of the situation, I immediately felt the tension leave and peace come. What a relief to be free of that tormenting worry because of my change of focus. Grasping the truth of the power of our words is life-changing and can mean the difference between victory and defeat.

The Philistine said to David, Come to me, and I will give your flesh to the birds of the air and the beasts of the field.

Then said David to the Philistine, You come to me with a sword, a spear, and a javelin, but I come to you in the name of the Lord of hosts, the God of the ranks of Israel, Whom you have defied.

This day the Lord will deliver you into my hand, and I will smite you and cut off your head. And I will give the corpses of the army of the Philistines this day to the birds of the air and the wild beasts of the earth, that all the earth may know that there is a God in Israel.

And all this assembly shall know that the Lord saves not with sword and spear; for the battle is the Lord's, and He will give you into our hands.

1 Samuel 17:44-47

Exercise Your Spiritual Authority

Speak To The Problem In The Name Of Jesus

All power has been given to the name of Jesus, and you, as a believer have been given that name (Philippians 2:9,10, John 16:23). Speak to the problem in the name of Jesus and command it to be gone from your household. Speak to whatever the enemy has sent your way that isn't lining up with God's will and Word. Sickness, strife, fear, and financial problems are all examples of problems that you can speak to in the name of Jesus and command to be gone from your home.

> **Truly I tell you, whoever says to this mountain, Be lifted up and thrown into the sea! and does not doubt at all in his heart but believes that what he says will take place, it will be done for him.**
>
> **Mark 11:23**

> **Behold! I have given you authority *and* power to trample upon serpents and scorpions, and [physical and mental strength and ability] over all the power that the enemy [possesses]; and nothing shall in any way harm you.**
>
> **Luke 10:19**

Bind and Loose

You have been given the authority to bind away evil and loose the power of God.

> **I tell you the truth, whatever you bind on earth will be bound in heaven, and whatever you loose on earth will be loosed in heaven.**
>
> **Matthew 18:18 (NIV)**

The same scripture from the Amplified Bible below adds clarity to the meaning of binding and loosing.

> **Truly I tell you, whatever you forbid and declare to be improper and unlawful on earth must be what is already forbidden in heaven, and whatever you permit and declare proper and lawful on earth must be what is already permitted in heaven.**
>
> **Matthew 18:18 (Amplified Bible)**

Bind fear and loose blood-covered peace in the name of Jesus (covered with the blood of Jesus that paid the price for your salvation and spiritual authority). Bind the sickness and loose blood-covered healing in the name of Jesus. Bind confusion and loose blood-covered wisdom and understanding in the name of Jesus. Bind a spirit of strife in the name of Jesus and loose blood-covered unity. Speak it and believe it.

It is called the good fight of faith (1 Timothy 6:12) because it truly is a fight. As you turn each situation over to the Lord, the Lord Himself will fight for you and He will enable you to transition to peace that defies what is going on around you as you focus on Him. What is good about this fight? You win! God declares in His Word that you are more than a conqueror and gain a surpassing victory through Him (Romans 8:37). He has provided us with the spiritual tools and knowledge through His Word to walk in victory.

Have A Right Heart

If there is sin in your hearts, your conscience will condemn you and you will not be able to come to the Lord in faith. Every day you need to ask the Lord to cleanse your heart and forgive you of any sins. Ask Him to show you where you have sin in your life. He will reveal to you where you need to make an attitude adjustment or ask for forgiveness. Living in a state of sin will block your prayers. As we team members prepare to minister to people coming with prayer needs at Guiding Light Ministries Healing Rooms, we begin our preparation time in our sanctuary praying and often, repenting. We ask God to cause us to have pure hearts before Him so there is nothing in us that would hinder the ministry that He wants to do through us to touch those coming for prayer. God is faithful to forgive and He chooses not to even remember our sin. When God convicts us of sin, the convicting draws us closer to Him so He can free us from the sin. But the enemy brings condemnation and that draws us away from God. God brings liberty. He wants us to be able to repent and move on!

> **If I regard iniquity in my heart, the Lord will not hear me.**
>
> **Psalm 66:18**

> **The Lord is far from the wicked, but He hears the prayer of the [consistently] righteous (the upright, in right standing with Him).**
>
> **Proverbs 15:29**

Unforgiveness will keep you stuck in the past and unable to move forward in many areas in your life, and your relationship with God is one of them. If we won't forgive, our Heavenly Father will not forgive us. To forgive is not at all to say that what happened to you wasn't wrong or hurtful. When you forgive, it frees you from the torment that holding a grudge brings and it releases the Lord to go in and deal with that other person. Forgive and ask the Lord to heal your hurt and entrust your feelings to Him so He can restore you to peace and wholeness.

> **For this reason I am telling you, whatever you ask for in prayer, believe (trust and be confident) that it is granted to you, and you will [get it].**
> **And whenever you stand praying, if you have anything against anyone, forgive him *and* let it drop (leave it, let it go), in order that your Father Who is in heaven may also forgive you your [own] failings and shortcomings and let them drop.**
> **But if you do not forgive, neither will your Father in heaven forgive your failings and shortcomings.**
>
> **Mark 11:24-26**

These scriptures identify some more specific behaviors that will block us from the blessings of God.

These six things the Lord hates, indeed, seven are an abomination to Him:
A proud look [the spirit that makes one overestimate himself and underestimate others], a lying tongue, and hands that shed innocent blood.
A heart that manufactures wicked thoughts *and* plans, feet that are swift in running to evil,
A false witness who breathes out lies [even under oath], and he who sows discord among his brethren.
Proverbs 6:16

Do not judge and criticize *and* condemn others, so that you may not be judged and criticized *and* condemned yourselves.
For just as you judge *and* criticize *and* condemn others, you will be judged and criticized and condemned, and in accordance with the measure you [use to] deal out to others, it will be dealt out again to you.
Matthew 7:1, 2

Ask the Lord to align you with Him in your heart. The Holy Spirit will show you your sin and give you the desire to be restored to Him. Repentance from the Lord is a gift! Repentance will cause your faith and peace to be renewed and you'll be ready to come boldly to His throne of grace. So get free! Though we fall, the Lord is faithful to pick us back up. He will always forgive us when we come with a humble and contrite heart and repent.

If we [freely] admit that we have sinned *and* confess our sins, He is faithful and just (true to His own nature and promises) and will forgive our sins [dismiss our lawlessness] and (continuously) cleanse us from all unrighteousness

[everything not in conformity to His will in purpose, thought, and action].

1 John 1:9

And beloved, if our consciences (our hearts) do not accuse us (if they do not make us feel guilty and condemn us), we have confidence (complete assurance and boldness) before God, ...

1 John 3:21

Connect To Other Believers

More times than I can count, the Lord has brought me from a state of feeling completely overwhelmed back to His peace and strength through ministry and prayers from other believers. You should not be isolated from the rest of the body. Even the Lone Ranger had Tonto! It isn't enough just to sit in the pews and receive the pastor's message and then go home and continue your Christian life by yourself. Through whatever avenues are open to you, get connected with some other Christian women who will pray with you and for you. Prayer support from the body of Christ can be the difference between victory and defeat. Having women prayer partners will help you grow in your faith. God will use that fellowship to enable you to go through some of life's rough spots and keep you on the path of life. Women's ministry activities or a Bible study are good possibilities for making these connections. If your husband is in church with you, look for a cell group or something that will connect you with other Christian couples. God has given His ministry gifts for your benefit. Sometimes just the right word from the Lord spoken through another believer hits the target in our hearts that can set us free from fear, despair or wrong thinking. Make yourself available to receive *and* give to the body. We are all meant to be vessels the Lord can pour His love and power into for others.

**And let us consider *and* give attentive, continuous care
to watching over one another, studying how we may stir up
(stimulate and incite) to love *and* helpful deeds *and* noble
activities.**

**Not forsaking *or* neglecting to assemble together [as
believers], as is the habit of some people, but admonishing
(warning, urging, and encouraging) one another, and all
the more faithfully as you see the day approaching.**

Hebrews 10:24, 25

To gain a surpassing victory, you must recognize your
complete dependency on the Lord. Jesus even has to supply
your faith. He is the author and finisher of it. Apart from Him,
you are unable to come to Him. You came because He wooed
you by His Holy Spirit. We in of ourselves have no power to
overcome or walk in victory. It's all through our union with
Him. It is through Him that we move from glory to glory.
Surrender to Him and put the full weight of your cares on Him.
The battle is now His.

Because of faith also Sarah herself received physical power to conceive a child, even when she was long past the age for it, because she considered [God] Who had given her the promise to be reliable and trustworthy and true to His word.

Hebrews 11:11

Chapter 3

God-Adventures That Deepened My Faith

God uses experiences in our lives when the odds look as if they are against us as opportunities to increase our faith. As we trust Him with a situation and we see His faithful provision, faith takes deeper root in our hearts. It isn't enough to know of His faithfulness just through reading the Bible. He means for us to know of His ability to turn a difficult circumstance into a victory through first-hand experience. Every time we share the testimony of His faithfulness in a given situation our faith roots grow deeper and our testimony waters the faith in the hearts of others. I call these times when God turns a difficult or impossible situation into a testimony of His miraculous power – a "God-adventure."

When the opportunity came into David's life to overcome Goliath, he had already been on some God-adventures that prepared his way for this miraculous victory. David was a slightly built young boy, but he was able to remember back to a time the Lord had empowered him to overcome a lion and later, God enabled him to take on a bear. God used these experiences to plant seeds of faith in David's heart. David knew that the same God that had given him victory over the lion and the bear would give him victory over the giant, Goliath. David also had developed a true *relationship* with God. The faith declaration he spoke to Goliath prophesying his victory over Goliath and the Philistine army came from Holy Spirit revelation of Who God is. They are the words of a believer who is walking by faith in his God and not by sight! They are the words of a man who has a revelation of the immeasurable *and* unlimited *and* surpassing greatness of God's power in and for us who believe, as demonstrated in the working of His mighty strength (Ephesians 1:19).

That is what God wants for you and me. As in Hebrews 11:11, He wants us to be able to consider Him reliable, trustworthy and true to His Word because there will be Goliaths in our paths. Through God, they can be overcome! In this chapter, are five God-adventures the Lord took me on to exercise and deepen my faith. By the time I was asking God to choose my husband, bring him to me and identify us to each other as husband and wife without any dating involved, I already knew Him as the God Who does the impossible. I considered Him reliable, trustworthy and true to His Word because God had watered my faith with the testimonies and teachings of Kenneth Hagin and Kenneth and Gloria Copeland. Then God started calling me out into the deep by taking me on my own God-adventures. The first adventure, *God Cares About Our Hearts' Desires,* happened four years before I asked God to be my match-maker. The second one, *Against All Odds,* happened around the start of my fourteen-year faith journey of waiting for my husband. The other three, *God Restores What Is Stolen, God Exposed What Was Hidden* and *I Can Do All Things Through Christ Who Strengthens Me* happened during the wait for my husband. God used these God-adventures as times to remind me that He is a personal God Who cares about the intimate details of our daily lives whether we are dealing with a relatively small loss on the grand scale of things, the attainment of a heart's desire or a heart-breaking trauma. With Him nothing is too small or too big! May your faith roots be watered and grow deeper from these stories of God's faithfulness in the following pages.

God Cares About Our Hearts' Desires

God says in Psalm 37:4 if we delight ourselves in Him, He will give us the desires and secret petitions of our hearts. God met a deep desire of my heart that many would consider frivolous and not worthy of God's attention. Many would say my desire was too self-focused and with so many really grievous situations in our world whether or not this desire was met was of no importance. God was not in that group of many! God did care. God graciously met me where I was, which at the time of this circumstance was in an immature state of Christianhood. The reality of my mindset was life was pretty much all about me. This God-adventure happened in 1984 when the knowledge of the power of our words, taking our spiritual authority and releasing a situation over to the Lordship of Jesus Christ had recently been planted in my heart. God took me on a God-adventure to water the faith roots of this baby Christian to let me know that what is important to me *is* important to Him and the spiritual principles I had been learning actually do work!

Lucerne, Switzerland, is a beautiful ancient town nestled by the Alps Mountains on Lake Lucerne. Its storybook charm had captivated my heart on two previous European vacations, and I was enthralled with every inch of it; the swans floating down the River Reuss as you sip your tea at a sidewalk café, the Swiss paintings on the old buildings, the fountains on cobblestone streets, the ancient wall surrounding the city with towers lit up at night and the wooden bridges people walk to cross the river were often in my thoughts.

I was in my late twenties. I wanted to be married but I wasn't. I wanted to have a house but I couldn't afford or want one by myself. I wanted to have a family but there was no husband! I wanted to be "normal" and have what it seemed like the whole rest of the world was having at this stage in their lives. I didn't have those things. But one thing I did have was my trips to Europe. Although wonderful and exciting beyond my wildest dreams, they were still in my mind a consolation prize for what I was missing. My three-month summer vacation that came with the job of teacher had allowed me to take wonderful trips: one to Hawaii for two weeks and two to Europe for three and then seven weeks. Now the "mother of all trips" was just ahead and I could barely sleep from the excitement of it. My friend Kathi and I were leaving for an eight-week trip that would take us all over Europe revisiting places we loved that allowed for more time on our own as well as exploring new territory. Centermost in our thoughts was the couple of days that would be spent in Lucerne. So intense was our adoration of this city, we would have paid the same for the tour, if the rest of the itinerary had been cancelled except for the time in Lucerne, had that been our only hope of a return. And we would not have considered the trip for any price had Lucerne been excluded from the itinerary.

Unlike previous trips, there were some unpleasant surprises on this one. I had grown to expect a high standard in accommodations on my vacations. Unlike the others, this was a student tour and what was described in the brochures in glowing terms was, to Kathi and me, very sub-standard and disappointing. But the shock that knocked us off our feet was learning just days after the start of the tour that rather than spending several days in Lucerne, we would be spending *one afternoon.* This was in no way acceptable and I realized from recent biblical teachings that *we were being robbed by the enemy!*

We quickly decided that we two would leave the tour and go on our own to spend several days in Lucerne. When our group left Venice, we would leave straight for Lucerne and skip a trip to Innsbruck, Austria, which we had already seen. Now, our job was to make reservations at the Hotel Balances in Lucerne for our stay. Arrangements for the train trip from Venice to Lucerne could be made through help from our tour company when we were in Venice. It sounded simple, but at every turn we were met with a wall of opposition! When we were in Paris, we found their phone system was light years behind ours in the U.S. and the only way to call a place in a foreign country was to make a trip to the library to use the phone there. (Remember, this was way before the time of cell phones.) We didn't have time to go to the library! It wasn't an option. Roadblocks similar to these were encountered on a daily basis for several weeks as we struggled to make contact with our hotel in Switzerland. The enemy was not going to win this one! I prayed and thanked God daily that He would make a way for that contact to happen and He would bring our long dreamed of return to Lucerne into a reality. Our tour mates understood and sympathized. After weeks of daily failed attempts, one day during a lunch stop I got the call through to the Hotel Balances and our reservations were made. God had brought the breakthrough! I cried tears of joy and relief upon hanging up the phone and when we boarded the bus and let our group know the connections had been made, the entire group let out a mighty yell of victory in response to our good turn of events.

As we enjoyed our trip leading up to Lucerne, we marveled every day that the greatest part of our adventure was just ahead. Our time in Venice was coming to a close. The train reservations for the trip from Venice to Milan, Italy, to Lucerne, Switzerland, were made. Arrangements were all set. We would leave our hotel at 6:00 am, walk to a taxi stop to take a canal boat to the train station and we would be on our way. After several days in Lucerne we would rejoin our tour when they came for the afternoon visit. We went to bed feeling like little children who can hardly contain themselves the night before Christmas. It was really happening!

The next morning we rose bright and early and by 5:30 am we were in the hotel lobby ready to start our walk to the taxi boat. The hotel building had at one time been a home for Catholic nuns and was surrounded by a wall which was locked at night but was to be unlocked early enough for Kathi and me to leave on time. As the time neared for us to leave, the woman who should have arrived to unlock the wall gate and man the desk was still not there. As we helplessly and somewhat aimlessly wandered around the lobby waiting for our release, Kathi partially stepped on the edge of a wooden platform which she hadn't noticed was raised several inches higher than the rest of the floor. On the wall above the platform was a wooden key rack holding dozens of sharp metal prongs turned upwards holding some keys. As she fell to the floor, her arm caught on some of the metal prongs, ripping it deep to the bone. The tear was horrendous!

The first words out of her mouth were, "Now we won't be able to go to Lucerne."

"Yes, we will!" I quickly said, determined to cancel the power of a negative declaration. God had placed us in a room that happened to be across from that of our young Austrian tour guide, Felix. Normally we wouldn't have any idea where his room would be, but after Kathi's fall I dashed upstairs, knocking on poor Felix's door at six in the morning with the news that Kathi had fallen and torn her arm open. Felix quickly dressed and walked Kathi to the hospital so her arm could be sewn up and bandaged.

From that point on for the next hour or so, a steady barrage of missiles from the enemy were launched out into the atmosphere and directed at our trip to Lucerne through the mouth of the tour company employee who was stationed in Venice for the summer. He talked about how dangerous it would be for Kathi to leave the tour with her arm in that condition and the many horrible scenarios that were likely to happen. His predictions of her pain, possible infection and lack of needed medical help because of our leaving the tour were just the beginning of his dire predictions.

He also said that there were probably no other trains to Lucerne from Venice that day and it would be extremely unwise for us to make any attempts to continue with our plans to separate from the tour group. I did not take these remarks as coming from a human being. I was polite but unresponsive. The enemy had been trying to rob us of our time in Lucerne since the start of the trip and this was the final battle! The spiritual teachings from the last few years continually rose up in my mind and a Holy Spirit anger at the enemy's continued interference with what to me was about to be a mighty blessing rose up in my spirit with a firm resolve to believe that God had heard my prayers and He was faithful. Faith seeds that had been planted in my heart took deeper root because of the intensity and desperation of the situation, and I experienced what had to be a gift of faith. Pictures of Kenneth Copeland standing over a difficult situation and pointing down to it declaring, "Jesus Is Lord!" as he taught on our authority as believers and of the power of the name of Jesus came flooding to my memory. I declared that Jesus was Lord over this trip and I spoke to the enemy in my mind with lips moving silently that he was defeated, and I praised God for His faithfulness and provision. I resolved to give no heed to the enemy's threats that our trip was out of the question. In spite of the fact that it appeared likely there were no more trains to Lucerne, this faith that came up in my heart said it didn't matter. None of these things mattered! God was not surprised by this chain of events and I absolutely knew His provision was already in place to enable us to overcome.

"All things are possible with God!" my spirit declared. God was my way-maker here and I was so fully persuaded beyond a shadow of a doubt that our trip was assured I wouldn't have been even the slightest bit surprised if a man who was really an angel walked in announcing that he was here to take us to Lucerne. In fact, I expected it! This gift of faith had lifted me out of all reach of any fear or discouragement. Being in that state of faith was exhilarating. All limitations were removed and the way was clear for us to move into victory! I was free from the natural and had moved into the supernatural realm! I knew the world would consider all this a ridiculous delusion, though it was as real to me as the hand at the end of my arm.

As I determined to hold on to the promises of God, I also determined to keep this faith battle to myself. There is a time to share and a time to keep quiet. Kathi had returned from the hospital, sewn up and bandaged from wrist to elbow. As we ate breakfast with our friends on the tour, they bemoaned the loss of our Lucerne adventure. I kept quiet, determined not to verbally agree with a bad report.

After breakfast a chain of events that was one amazing blessing after another linked together to become the most wonderful adventure to Lucerne that could have been hoped for. It began with the news that rather than having to make a change of trains in Milan, we could take a train from Venice at 11:00 am that would go non-stop to Lucerne. Our train trip was on one of those old-styled trains we see in the movies with little individual compartments and bench-styled seats facing each other. Our cabin mates were a sweet Italian couple and her sister who was also on her way to Lucerne. They spoke no English, but several years of intense study of Italian enabled me to poorly say just about anything and understand them enough to get the main ideas. We happily discussed all the wonderful attributes of our destination and they expressed their concern for Kathi's arm and suggested some things she may want to purchase at a pharmacy in Lucerne. It was a delightful eight-hour ride. Kathi's arm *never hurt* at that time or at any other part of our adventure and needless to say there was no infection. As our train pulled into the station, Kathi and I were amazed to see the largest most beautiful and complete rainbow expanding from the ground on one side of the rainbow to the ground on its other side. It was God's personal sign to us that said, "Be blessed, girls! This trip is on me!" It brought tears to my eyes at this clear reminder of how He loves us.

Every moment of the stay in Lucerne fulfilled every hope we had had and more. In spite of the fact we had so recently made our reservations, God had given us one of the best rooms with a view on the river side of the hotel. We ate our breakfasts on our balcony facing the Alps Mountains overlooking the River Reuss and the beautiful cathedral on the other side. We walked along the tower walls and visited the dying lion and every favorite spot as well as new ones. Our required trip to the hospital for a quick change of bandages for Kathi was on our way to places we wanted to go. We once again took the evening cruise on Lake Lucerne with the city's lights reflecting on the lake and song of the alpine horn with its echo coming from the Alps becoming part of a moving melody.

I knew I had been on a God-adventure. My life would never be the same. Faith seeds had grown roots and I had experienced seeing some of God's spiritual principles at work first hand. Even as I relive this experience, my faith roots grow deeper from the memory of it and I am once again filled with awe at how great is the Father's willingness to meet our hearts' desires if we will believe.

When I returned from my European vacation and pondered God's provision on the trip to Lucerne, with thanksgiving to the Lord, I wrote this poem so I would never forget.

Cowbells…….. in the distance I hear their jingle.
Alps and quaint Swiss houses intermingle.
Luscious green mountains, white houses, roofs red,
Flowers in window boxes, Let it be said
That we're on our way to Lucerne!

A dying stone lion tugs at the heart
Colorful buildings with charming Swiss art
Old wooden bridges, Dance of the Dead
As the River Reuss flows, Let it be said,
That there is no place like Lucerne.

Sidewalk cafes, swans serenely float by,
Alpine horn echoes its song in the sky.
As it bounces off mountains, man and nature come together.
With a lump in our throats, we don't know whether
It's a wonderful dream or Lucerne.

Lights dance on the lake and shine in a tower.
Oh magic Lucerne, you do have the power
To give us sweet memories we'll often relive.
We love all the beauty and joy that you give.
Thank you, thank you, Lucerne.

All praise be to God for that trip to Lucerne!
He answers our prayers for what we most yearn.
When we plug in our faith things must make a turn.
Thank you, Lord, for Lucerne.

Against All Odds

Every God-adventure will equip you to believe God more easily and give you a deeper revelation of some facet of His wonderful personality. After the trip to Lucerne it was forever settled in my heart that God cares about meeting our hearts' desires. God used this new faith in my heart to meet the desires of another, which is *always* His plan. Freely have we received, freely we are to give (Matthew 10:8)!

In 1988, Katie was a twenty-year-old girl in my church who deeply wanted to get her G.E.D. Being mentally challenged, she had always been in classes for special needs students. Because of teasing from her peers she had dropped out of school in her sophomore year and had been robbed of the blessing of a high school diploma which she much regretted. When she mentioned to me that she really wanted to study to get her G.E.D., the Holy Spirit prompted me to volunteer to be her tutor.

God used another lesson from Kenneth Copeland to prepare me for this task. I saw Kenneth tell of an incident on his television show when a parachute had its cords accidently pulled with such power, the knots that were in each of its three cords had been completely flattened to an almost smooth texture. The level of tightness in the knots made it impossible for human beings to get them out by using their natural abilities. Kenneth and another believer each picked up a knot, laid it across one of their palms and began speaking to the knot to come out in the name of Jesus as they lightly stroked the knot with their pointer fingers. Their fingers brushing across the surface of the knots accomplished absolutely nothing, but they were taking the action of faith as they commanded the knots to loosen in Jesus' name. As they spoke in the name of Jesus, the knots loosened. Even the knot on the third cord that lay on the ground began to loosen. Because of the power released at the name of Jesus and their faith in that name, the impossible was accomplished as they took actions of faith.

Katie and I met in my kitchen every Wednesday and Thursday from 4:00 pm to 7:00 pm. She had brought over the five thick books holding the information that she was to learn and master in order to pass the tests. Those books sat in my apartment for the duration of the time she prepared for the test, as my home was the only place in which she studied. Only one of those books was ever opened and that was the one covering the subject of English. Every study session without exception, began with a prayer of thanksgiving to God that Katie would pass her G.E.D. Then we studied for as long as Katie's attention span would allow, which was about thirty minutes. The rest of the time we would talk, fix supper and share the evening meal. Each week, we went over almost the same material because what had been learned the week before hadn't been retained. We were as Kenneth Copeland and his friend running their fingers over the knots. Nothing was being accomplished through Katie's natural abilities to get prepared for the tests. But we were taking the action of faith and doing what we could do as we believed for God to do the rest. After a year and a half of preparation, Katie took her G.E.D. and passed *every section* the very *first* time she was tested! When Katie called to say that she had passed the tests, she mentioned that she had also had to take the Constitution test which she didn't even know was required and she had passed that too! I had failed the Constitution test the first time I had taken it in college and I had studied!

It was with great joy that Katie's parents and I sat in the stands at her G.E.D. graduation and watched her proudly receive her diploma. With God all things are possible!

God Restores What Is Stolen

God was about to take me on another adventure but I didn't know it. I thought I was just going to the Shop N' Save to get my next week's supply of groceries. This particular shopping excursion occurred sometime in the early 90s. As usually happened, I realized that there was an item on my list that I had overlooked a few rows back and I left my cart in an out of the way spot as I usually did, to walk back to find the forgotten item. The one thing that was not usual about this trip was that I didn't have my purse with the soft strap that I normally kept safely on my shoulder. It was summer time, and I had recently bought a big straw purse with some needlework on one side displaying a large turquoise hummingbird. The handle was wooden and not as long as my usual purse strap. Because of the discomfort of wearing the hummingbird purse on my shoulder, I had set it in the basket at the front of the grocery cart. I wasn't accustomed to having to keep the cart with me or having to remember that my purse needed watching, so when I realized I needed to backtrack, I went into automatic and did what I always did, leaving the cart unattended. When I returned I added the last item to the rest of my groceries and started to continue shopping. After just a few steps I came to the horrible realization that my purse *was missing*! Inside my purse was enough cash for a large shopping trip, my checkbook, all my credit cards and keys.

Trying to remain calm and think what I should do, I headed for the customer service desk to report the crime. When I got to the desk, there was a line of four or five customers in front of me. It was then, as I started my wait in line, that the same Holy Spirit anger that came up in my spirit when the trip to Lucerne looked like it was lost, came up again and God transformed me instantaneously from a victim to a victor! Silently I began to pray for God to rescue me and thanked Him that my purse and everything in it would be returned. I prayed that a holy fear of the Lord would fall upon the person who had taken it. I prayed the thief would be absolutely desperate not only to be free of it, but also to do whatever was necessary to get it back into my hands. Then in the name of Jesus, I bound the enemy and started praising God for His help. I didn't know if my belongings would be returned in five minutes or five days but my faith said it was a done deal.

When it was finally my turn at the desk, I gave them a description of my purse and five young male employees fanned the store looking for it. One thing that made the search easy was that probably no one else had a big straw purse with a turquoise hummingbird on the side. After several minutes, one of the young men walked up holding my purse in his hands asking if this was it. He said it had been in the basket of an empty cart sitting by itself at the front of the store beyond the check-out lines. Upon examining my purse contents I saw that nothing was missing! My cash, my checkbook, credit cards and keys had been untouched. God had protected me!

There have been several other incidents when God has had me pray in that same way that His Holy Spirit fear would come upon people to the extent they would be afraid to do anything but what is right. I knew in my spirit, on one occasion He was keeping me safe from harm through that prayer. Although my straw purse is old and probably not much of a fashion statement, I keep it as a tangible reminder that God protects and restores what has been stolen! And once in a while in the summer, I carry it and relish the opportunity to share what God did for me and will do for any who would look to Him for help in their time of need.

God Exposed What Was Hidden

It was a snowy winter night in December, in the mid 90s. I was curled up on my couch finishing the last of my Christmas cards when I realized that I was one short. This card needed to go to one of my first grade students from long ago. This little gal had started inviting me to her sporting events when she was in junior high and high school. I had attended her high school graduation and been invited to her home to celebrate her graduation from college as well. She had grown into a beautiful Christian woman, and I enjoyed our continued yearly communications in our Christmas cards. Because the shopping area was just blocks from my neighborhood, I decided to run out to the nearby Christian bookstore to get her card. Shortly after returning home, I noticed that one of the gold earrings that I had worn to the store was missing. It was a flat broadband hoop of polished gold that I had gotten from QVC, one of my favorite pairs. Because it was real gold and not costume jewelry, I wasn't willing to just let it go and call it lost. I really felt that it was in the parking lot of the shopping center. So I started praying that God would protect the earring so it wouldn't be run over or picked up by some other shopper. I prayed that He would open my eyes so my attention would be directed to the right spot as He ordered my steps to its location.

As the snowflakes continued to twirl from the sky, I drove back to the shopping center. I didn't know exactly where I had parked before, but thought I knew the row. Parking farther down than I had on the first trip, I got out of my car and started looking. Although the lot was full of cars belonging to Christmas shoppers, the spot where I thought I may have previously parked was empty and had a covering of snow that glistened under the parking lot lights. As my eyes scanned the snow, a tiny glint of gold caught my eye. A very tiny spec of edge of the gold band was visible through the snow. So small was the amount of gold showing, it would have gone undetected by anyone who wasn't looking for something in particular. It was my earring! With all the in and out travel in the row of cars where it lay, my earring had gone undetected and had been kept out of the path of car wheels. Many years and earring purchases later, it is still my favorite pair.

There have been other times I have asked God to open my eyes to see something that has been lost. The item has often been found lying out in the open, where surely I should have seen it the first time I looked. No concern of ours is too small for our Heavenly Father to address. I believe far too often, what has been lost or stolen is never recovered because we haven't thought to ask Him for His help.

I Can Do All Things Through Christ Who Strengthens Me

My father had been a rock in my life, on whom I could always depend. As a child he had been my protector, provider and teacher. He taught me to value the ability to persevere under difficult circumstances and do what is right regardless of the price that may need to be paid. I can recall many seemingly casual conversations with him when I knew the real purpose of his words was to impart wisdom or to develop character. He was a man who was never ashamed to tell his family he loved them. He was fiercely loyal to those he loved and a man of great integrity. He had been my school principal in elementary school and he had cheered me on as I entered my teaching career. Even at the age of 40 I was still his little girl and he was my daddy.

In his later years I had shared my Kenneth Copeland tapes and Kenneth Hagin books with him and he had devoured them all. He had been raised in the Presbyterian church and was a faithful church goer, but until his later years, he had never completely understood the salvation message that we are saved through grace by faith in Jesus Christ. With his development of a true personal relationship with Jesus, came a very disciplined prayer life and he daily spent time in the Word. I also recall him commenting that should the time ever come that he was unable to do his daily prayers it was likely that "all hell would break loose." This story is probably a good lesson on why we need to watch our words because with the onslaught of his heart problems he was unable to pray and just as his words had predicted, some hellish events took place.

"I can do all things through Christ Who strengthens me!" (Philippians 4:13) were familiar words I had heard him emphatically say on numerous occasions. Any time I heard or read that scripture he would come to mind, as it was one of his favorites.

In August of 1996, while mowing the lawn, my dad experienced a heart attack that caused extreme damage to his heart. Later that month he had open heart surgery at age 72. It seemed that everything that could go wrong had been going wrong, but at least he was still alive. After the initial operation, his heart wasn't strong enough to enable him to breathe on his own, so he had continued to have to rely on the breathing tube which is so uncomfortable that patients have to be pretty much sedated all the time to tolerate it. After a week or so of being continuously attached to the breathing tube, my dad's wires that were holding the recently stitched up parts in his chest together, had loosened from too much movement as he struggled in and out of consciousness. The surgeon had to operate again to rewire his bones.

Something happened during that second surgery and when he eventually was able to breathe on his own, we found that his brain had been injured and he no longer knew who any of us were. I was no longer the apple of his eye. He knew my mother, my brother or me no better than a fly on the wall. The usual recognition and love was gone from his eyes and he spoke no more than a word or two at a time. He had to be taught to learn everything all over again. Even swallowing was a monumental task.

When asked simple questions like, "Do you like blueberries?" (which he loved) or "Do you have any grandchildren?" he gave the wrong answers. My dad's body was functioning but my dad was gone. For six weeks, he knew nothing of our presence although we were there with him. I remember one Sunday afternoon, he was sitting in the hospital hallway outside of his room. I was in a chair next to him and I think he didn't even notice that a person or chair was there. I continued to pray for him as I had been doing daily and believed for his full recovery.

The next day when I came home from teaching school, my mother called with news of *the miracle*. My mother had been in the hospital room with my dad and some nurses. He was in what had become his usual state of no recognition of the familiar and inability to carry on anything close to a normal thought process. He had never spoken a well-developed sentence since the brain injury. Then, out of the blue, words that belonged together came up from his spirit and out his mouth and formed this powerful declaration of God's Word, *"I can do all things through Christ Who strengthens me!"*

God immediately began performing His Word that my dad had spoken! Mental abilities began rapidly returning to my father's brain and within the hour he was my dad again! He knew who he was and he knew us. Christ had strengthened his weak mind and through Christ, my dad was thinking and speaking with restored ability. The hospital personnel were amazed to say the least! God had done a miracle! The enemy had had him bound but through the power of His Word, Jesus Christ had made him free. That scripture that had grown such deep faith roots in his heart had risen right up out of my dad's spirit without any help from his brain. God had watched over His Word to perform it!

Then said the Lord to me, You have seen well, for I am alert *and* active, watching over My word to perform it.

Jeremiah 1:12

Afterword

Whether you are a single or married woman, the solution to the problem that leads you to ask the question, *What about my husband, Lord?* is the same! Put it in God's hands and let Him take care of it. Cast your cares on Him! In both situations, the enemy is trying to get you to carry a burden that is not yours. If your eyes are not on Jesus, if you are not entrusting Him with your situation, you will take matters into your own hands to try to bring about the desired outcome. That behavior won't get you the results you so desire.

Stop striving! God has the perfect plan for you. Whatever your circumstances, God is ready to turn the tide and transform your situation into a God-adventure. As God's child, you are meant to be a victor not a victim! Draw near to God and allow Him to give you the grace to turn it all over to Him and you will be able to walk in peace. It will no longer be your problem but your Heavenly Father's problem! Daughter, He is longing for you to let Him meet all your needs! All things are possible with God; His name is Faithful and True (Revelation 19:11).

For with God nothing is ever impossible *and* no word from God shall be without power *or* impossible of fulfillment.

Luke 1:37

And blessed (happy, to be envied) is she who believed that there would be a fulfillment of the things that were spoken to her from the Lord.

Luke 1:45

Endnotes

1. Derek Prince with Ruth Prince, <u>God Is A Match-Maker</u> (Charlotte, North Carolina: Chosen books, 1986).

2. John Eldredge, <u>Wild At Heart</u> (Nashville, Tennessee: Thomas Nelson Inc., 2001) 9, 48.

Favorite Books God Used To Teach Me His Ways

Copeland, Gloria, *And Jesus healed them all* (Fort Worth: KCP Publications, 1984).

Copeland, Gloria, *God's Will Is Prosperity* (Fort Worth: KCP Publications, 1978).

Copeland, Kenneth, *freedom from fear* (Fort Worth: Kenneth Copeland Publications, 1980).

Hagin, Kenneth E., *Casting Your Cares Upon The Lord* (Tulsa: Faith Library Publications, 1981).

Hagin, Kenneth E., *the name of JESUS* (Tulsa: Faith Library Publications, 1979).

Hagin, Kenneth E., *Seven Things You Should Know About Divine Healing* (Tulsa: Faith Library Publications, 1979).

Hagin, Kenneth E., *Turning Hopeless Situations Around* (Tulsa: Faith Library Publications, 1981).

Hagin, Kenneth E., *What To Do When Faith Seems Weak & Victory Lost* (Tulsa: Faith Library Publications, 1979).

Hagin, Kenneth E., *WORDS* (Tulsa: Faith Library Publications, 1985).

Hayes, Norvel, *How To Live And Not Die* (Tulsa: Harrison House, 1986).

Hinn, Benny, *Good Morning, Holy Spirit* (Nashville: Thomas Nelson Publishers, 1990).

Meyer, Joyce, *Battlefield Of The Mind* (Tulsa: Harrison House, 2002).

Meyer, Joyce, *"Me and My Big Mouth!"* (Tulsa: Harrison House, 1997).

Mize, Jackie, *Supernatural Childbirth: Experiencing the Promises of God Concerning Conception and Delivery* (Tulsa: Harrison House, 1995).

Parsley, Rod, *No More Crumbs* (Lake Mary, FL: Creation House, 1997).

Prince, Derek with Ruth Prince, *God Is A Match-Maker* (Grand Rapids, MI: Chosen Books, 1986).

Savelle, Jerry, *Giving Birth To A Miracle* (Tulsa: Harrison House, 1981).

Savelle, Jerry, *If Satan Can't Steal Your Joy... He Can't Keep Your Goods* (Tulsa: Harrison House, 1982).

Wigglesworth, Smith, *Ever Increasing Faith* (Springfield, MO: Gospel Publishing House, 1924).

Word Ministries, Inc., *Prayers That Avail Much: An Intercessor's Handbook of Scriptural Prayers* (Tulsa: Harrison House, 1980).

Word Ministries, Inc., *Prayers That Avail Much: An Intercessor's Handbook of Scriptural Prayers, Volume Two* (Tulsa: Harrison House, 1989).

Word Ministries, Inc., *Prayers That Avail Much: An Intercessor's Handbook of Scriptural Prayers, Volume Three* (Tulsa: Harrison House, 1997).

CPSIA information can be obtained at www.ICGtesting.com
Printed in the USA
LVOW042058170912

299184LV00001B/2/P